"The Journey Inward Begins with Silence"

"The Journey Inward Begins with Silence"

Sitting With Your Thoughts

A Journey Into the Mind, Spirit, and Self

FORSHADOWING

Sitting With Your Thoughts is a journey of 27 chapters that guides the reader from mental chaos to spiritual stillness. Beginning with internal wars, demonic whispers, childhood wounds, and emotional confusion, Malik courageously faces each layer of his mind and soul. Every chapter introduces a new truth, a new layer of self to examine. The structure—a combination of narrative reflection, spiritual seeking, and practical action—helps readers mirror their own healing. From the awakening of faith to the revelation of divine identity, this book ends not with answers, but with presence. True transformation isn't loud—it's the quiet that finally makes sense. And this book, above all, teaches you how to listen to that quiet.

SENSITIVE CONTENT WARNING

"The Journey Inward Begins with Silence"

Table of Contents

"The Journey Inward Begins with Silence"

--- PART II — THE UNVEILING ---

--- PART III — THE RETURN TO SELF ---

"The Journey Inward Begins with Silence"

About the Author

Malik is a visionary writer, truth-seeker, and spiritual architect born and raised in Los Angeles, California. With a natural leadership spirit and a deeply rooted passion for transformation, Malik channels his life experiences—from inner battles to divine awakenings—into powerful, reflective storytelling. His ability to balance raw honesty with higher insight invites readers into deep self-examination and healing. When he's not writing, Malik continues pursuing his passion in architecture, with

"The Journey Inward Begins with Silence"

dreams of building not just structures—but safe havens
for the mind and spirit

.

Author's Reflection

Writing this book wasn't just a process—it was a
breakthrough. Every chapter pulled from the depths of my
experiences, some painful, some powerful, but all
necessary. I didn't write this as someone who figured it all
out—I wrote it as someone who decided to sit still long
enough to listen. Through trauma, forgiveness, fatherhood,
faith, and silence, I found my true voice. If you're holding
this book, I want you to know—you're not alone in your
thoughts. And if you're still searching, that means you still
believe there's more. This was my journey home to self. I
hope it leads you to yours too.

—Malik

"The Journey Inward Begins with Silence"

CHAPTER ONE

Voice in the Dark

<u>The Seeker</u>

Have you ever heard a voice in your head that didn't feel like your own?

Not the voice you use to plan or imagine—but the one that whispers guilt, commands action, or questions your worth. The voice that doesn't ask—it intrudes. It doesn't guide—it manipulates.

We all have conversations with our thoughts. But what if those conversations weren't always with ourselves?

"The Journey Inward Begins with Silence"

In this war between silence and chaos, most people don't realize they've been listening to an enemy disguised as their inner voice.

The Mirror

Voice of the Devil

I'm starting to question everything I thought I knew.

Everything in existence is made up of cells—so small, you can't see them with the naked eye. And yet, each one holds a purpose, a function, a task. A single human on Earth is no different. We're small, but meaningful. We exist to create or help. That's the core of humanity—creation or service. Some do both. Most do neither.

"The Journey Inward Begins with Silence"

We fear death. But the more I sit with it, the more I understand—there is no death, not in the way we think. When the body dies, you enter a deeper consciousness. One where every unanswered question finds clarity. You transition. You begin again.

You're born into a new body, forgetting the life you left behind. But pieces return. A face you recognize but never met. A memory that doesn't belong to this timeline. These fragments bleed into your new story like dreams with roots you can't trace.

We are electrical beings. A unified current of awareness. God is not above us—God is within. And if God is within, then we are not separate from Him.

"The Journey Inward Begins with Silence"

You are a part of God. Which means, in essence—you are divine.

But here's the deception: the voice you listen to... the one that drives you toward fear, anger, destruction—it isn't yours. It isn't God's either. It is a voice that wears your tone and steals your name.

So fight.

Not for your ego. Not for your country.

Fight for your consciousness.

The Guide

War on Thoughts

"The Journey Inward Begins with Silence"

Words hold power. Speak something with conviction—something rooted in belief—and it changes how people see the world. It can change how you see it, too.

Thoughts echo across time. The past reminds you, "You should've done this." The future whispers, "You will do that." But neither speaks with your true voice. The commands come fast, disguised as decisions, and before you know it, you're following orders that feel like your own—but aren't.

That's how the war begins. Quietly. Silently. Within.

In joy, you know not to hurt yourself. But in depression, that same wisdom disappears. Why?

Because the voice of destruction is loudest when the soul is quiet.

"The Journey Inward Begins with Silence"

We hear thoughts all day long. We follow commands without realizing they weren't born from us. And yet, no scan, no machine, no physician can locate a single thought inside the body.

So ask yourself: if you can't explain how you create a thought, are you really the one creating them?

Where do emotions live in your body?

Can you point to the origin of jealousy?

Can you dissect guilt?

We've been tricked into believing we are the thinkers.

But sometimes... we are just the listeners.

"The Journey Inward Begins with Silence"

Sit With This Thought

• Have you ever done something you later swore "wasn't really you"? Who—or what—do you think it was?

• How much of your inner dialogue truly belongs to you?

• What thoughts today felt more like commands than choices?

Try This Within

Silence Practice (15 minutes):

Sit in total silence and simply observe your thoughts. No judgment. Just watch. When a thought comes, ask: Did I create this—or just receive it?

Name the Voice (3-Day Challenge):

"The Journey Inward Begins with Silence"

For three days, carry a notebook or phone note. Every time a strong inner command arises (positive or negative), write it down. Label it:

• Self

• Spirit

• Other

At the end of three days, study the pattern. Which voice are you following the most?

CHAPTER TWO

Shadow Games

The Seeking

"The Journey Inward Begins with Silence"

Have you ever been scared of your own mind?

Not from what someone said or did, but from what you thought might happen. A sound outside. A look from someone you love. A voice in your head that turns your peace into paranoia. That fear you feel? That dread? That's not always you. That's not always real.

Sometimes it's not just what's happening around you—it's who's trying to speak through your thoughts.

And sometimes... the devil doesn't come with horns.

He comes as you.

The Mirror

"The Journey Inward Begins with Silence"

Drugged Story

I had a crazy moment—one I'll never forget.

I was smoking, just trying to relax, when suddenly everything shifted. I looked up at the ceiling fan and watched it twist into the face of Satan. Not a feeling—his actual face. In the flesh. Hovering, watching, leaning in. I couldn't feel my legs. I couldn't move. I wasn't myself.

The last thing I remember before I slipped was my girlfriend's voice saying, "Don't tell anyone this story."

Then it was like I snapped back into my body—but everything had changed.

"The Journey Inward Begins with Silence"

Weed opened a door. And something dark walked through.

The moment I relaxed, I turned into someone else. My words changed. My actions weren't mine. I slipped into this fog where my body stayed, but my mind left. I remember shaking. I remember everything from the waist down becoming sensitive and foreign. I remember being terrified—and paralyzed.

And then came the guilt.

The shame of not knowing what I had said. The fear of seeing her angry. The voice in my head trying to convince me I did something unforgivable. But that wasn't me. That wasn't my soul speaking—that was something else using my voice.

I've come to realize something simple, but powerful:

"The Journey Inward Begins with Silence"

The effects of drugs don't just enhance the mind—they amplify the enemy.

That wasn't my reflection I was trapped inside. That was Satan. And he knows exactly what he's doing.

The Guide

Emotional Temptation

If you think something—but don't do it—does the thought still count?

"The Journey Inward Begins with Silence"

Tonight, I smoked. And as I sat there, I saw her face, panicked, calling me:

"That dude right there just robbed me!"

I looked up, saw someone running. "The one in white?" I asked.

Then I blinked—and snapped out of it.

None of it happened. She was fine. But my thoughts were trying to convince me otherwise.

That I should worry. That I should react. That I should fear something that hadn't even occurred.

Later that night, I prayed. As I prayed, demonic beasts circled around me in my mind—dark, snarling creatures trying to stir fear in me. But then I felt it... a divine force field. It wrapped around me and my son. I knew it was God. I knew He was keeping those spirits from touching us.

Still, they tried.

And still—I didn't give in.

Later, as I slept, chaos unfolded outside. A party nearby turned violent. Yelling. Arguing. Talk of guns. Of shooting. Of death. Satan was using others to keep me awake, to plant fear, to convince me that my son and I weren't safe.

But I adjusted to reality. I grabbed protection. I kept my son close. And I slept.

Fear only lives where faith is absent.

"The Journey Inward Begins with Silence"

And I'm learning this:

Your thoughts can create fear. But fear has no power once you realize it's only a shadow.

You can't predict the future. So why assume the worst?

Sit With This Thought

• Has your mind ever made you feel unsafe—even when nothing was happening?

• Can you tell the difference between a fear that's real and one that's imagined?

• Who are you when your mind runs wild—do you lose yourself, or meet your shadow?

Try This Within

"The Journey Inward Begins with Silence"

Midnight Anchor:

Next time fear creeps in at night—pause. Place one hand on your chest and speak this aloud:

"I am safe. I am here. This is my mind, and I belong to no other voice but God's."

Thought vs. Reality Check:

Any time you feel fear, stop and ask yourself:

• What's happening in my head?

• What's happening in front of my eyes?

If they don't match, choose what's real.

CHAPTER THREE

"The Journey Inward Begins with Silence"

Pretty Lies, Ugly Truths

<u>The Seeking</u>

What if the devil didn't just whisper... but watched?

Not from a distance. Not through temptation alone—but through mirrors. Dreams. Childhood echoes.

What if his presence showed up in the form of familiar rooms, familiar faces... and even familiar fear?

Sometimes the scariest things don't happen outside of you— they happen when you close your eyes.

What you feel in a dream can shake you in real life.

"The Journey Inward Begins with Silence"

And what you bury in childhood can rise like smoke through a memory.

The devil doesn't always attack with sound.

Sometimes, he shows you things.

<u>The Mirror</u>

Devil's Presents

I remember the times I slipped into comas—deep ones. Not medical, but spiritual.

It would happen after only 30 minutes to an hour of rest. I'd close my eyes, and when I opened them, I wasn't in the same world. I remember getting up, walking to the bathroom next to my bedroom. Everything felt normal. I used the toilet. Flushed. Went to the sink.

Then I looked in the mirror.

Words were written on it—in red marker, but I didn't write them.

It said: "I want your soul."

Terror froze my body. I realized I was inside a nightmare. I ran out of the bathroom, heart pounding, but no matter what room I ran to—the hallway, the living room—they all turned into that same bathroom. Over and over.

It was like something was making it clear:

"The Journey Inward Begins with Silence"

"We're not done. We're still here. We're after you."

I woke up on the couch—but I couldn't move. My eyes were open, but my body was locked.

All around me was darkness, except for the shadow in front of me. It stood over me, still and silent, staring through my body like it had been waiting.

All I could do was scream in my mind.

I could feel sweat dripping down my face, my heart racing faster than I could count. That presence fed off my fear. It didn't speak. It didn't need to.

It was terror in form.

"The Journey Inward Begins with Silence"

Then something shifted. I stopped fighting. I relaxed. I whispered a prayer in my mind. I accepted that God was bigger than whatever this was. Slowly, the paralysis faded. The figure vanished. The thoughts went quiet.

But even after I woke up—I didn't sleep again that night. And for nights after… the episodes returned.

<u>The Guide</u>

The Dreamer

Some memories don't feel real—but they still carry pain.

I had a vision recently. A scene I couldn't tell was real or not. My dad asked me, "Who are you more scared of—me or your mom?" His eyes locked onto mine, fire behind them. I swallowed hard and pointed at him. He told me to come over.

"The Journey Inward Begins with Silence"

Then he punched me.

My mom told him, "You're going to traumatize him," but he just laughed while I cried—and she watched.

I don't know if that really happened. But it feels like it did.

I've learned something strange: when I write… sometimes the voices stop. Like they don't want me exposing them.

Yesterday I had a daydream—violent, painful. I saw myself choking and hitting my own son.

I'd never do that. I know I wouldn't. But the thought came. The emotion followed. Then the guilt wrapped around me.

"The Journey Inward Begins with Silence"

It wasn't me. But it was shown to me. And that matters.

Later, I stood in the bathroom, brushing my teeth. I looked into the mirror—but something felt off.

It wasn't me looking back. Not exactly. It was like my reflection was studying me, not mirroring me.

Behind me was the door, but my reflection's attention wasn't on that. It was on me.

Every time I pass a mirror now, I feel it.

A flicker of anxiety. A wave in my stomach.

Not because I don't know who I am—but because I know what's been watching.

"The Journey Inward Begins with Silence"

Forgiveness is key.

Not just for what was done—but for the fear I inherited.

Because if I can feel this way about myself…

I can only imagine how others see me.

<u>Sit With This Thought</u>

• Have you ever questioned whether a memory was real—but still felt the pain anyway?

• What's the last thing you saw in a dream or reflection that shook you awake?

• How many of your fears are inherited—not created?

<u>Try This Within</u>

Mirror Moment (3-Minute Practice):

"The Journey Inward Begins with Silence"

Stand in front of a mirror in silence. Look directly into your eyes.

When fear or shame rises, ask: "What part of me is afraid to be seen?"

Then whisper: "I forgive you."

Dream Watcher Journal:

Each time you dream something unsettling, write down:

• What happened

• What emotion came with it

• What memory (real or imagined) it triggered

Over time, you'll begin to see patterns—not just from the enemy, but from yourself seeking healing.

"The Journey Inward Begins with Silence"

CHAPTER FOUR

Facing Reality

The Seeking

What if the voice in your head isn't you at all?

Most people never question the thoughts that come to them. They believe every whisper must be their own. Every emotion must be true. Every command must be acted on.

But what if that voice was an imposter?

What if your greatest battles weren't between you and the world—but between your soul and something pretending to be your mind?

"The Journey Inward Begins with Silence"

Sometimes, reality isn't what you see.

It's what you discern.

The Mirror

Facing Reality

I've come to a hard truth:

The voice in my head isn't always mine.

It's the devil—pretending. He copies my tone, slips into my emotions, uses "I" to sound like me. But emotion is his identity. And deception is his game.

"The Journey Inward Begins with Silence"

He talks. I follow. But I'm learning to separate my soul from his tricks.

It's like poker. Life is just a table full of cards. You don't control what's dealt—but you control what you keep. If the hand in front of you doesn't serve you, fold it. Let it go. If it's something you can bear, accept it—but never confuse it for identity.

Too many of us hold on to what we should've discarded just because it came to us.

We need to learn how to sit still. No thoughts. No analysis.

Just stillness. Eyes closed. Breath deep.

When you do, you might feel a shiver. A slow rock inside your body.

That's not fear.

"The Journey Inward Begins with Silence"

That's not weakness.

That's your soul praying without words. That's your spirit touching the divine.

Don't let the left hand know what the right hand is doing. That old saying means more than action—it means don't let your thoughts betray your spirit.

When you speak in your head, you're not always speaking to yourself.

The devil listens. And he answers.

So I've started paying attention.

To the thoughts that say "you" instead of "I."

To the ones that talk to me, not from me.

"The Journey Inward Begins with Silence"

Every future-based thought that whispers what I should do?

It's already trying to persuade me—to shift me from peace into action I never chose.

But just like the bad thoughts come, the good ones arrive too.

And when they do, I write.

Because even what I write… is starting to reveal truth back to me.

The Guide

Fate of Faith

I'm realizing something beautiful now:

"The Journey Inward Begins with Silence"

The good things from God don't shout.

They don't stir up emotion or force movement. They feel like light—steady and soft.

They don't carry a feeling. They carry a presence.

Today I prayed. I didn't say much. I just sat. And in that stillness, I felt peace.

That's how I knew the Lord was with me.

I let the random thoughts come, and for once—I didn't follow any of them.

They faded before they could grow. I forgot them just as fast as they arrived.

Then a memory surfaced. A writing I had once asked about in prayer.

"Are these revelations?" I had asked.

"The Journey Inward Begins with Silence"

"Yes," another moment had answered, almost in the same breath.

The feelings I once had when thinking of my mom are gone now.

But strangely, I feel those same emotions now when I think of my dad.

It's like trauma takes turns wearing different faces.

And the scariest part is...

You don't always know you're not yourself.

What controls you is the thought of doing. Whether good or bad, it's still a thought.

And thoughts can't be controlled.

"The Journey Inward Begins with Silence"

But God can be trusted.

And faith… is the filter that keeps you from moving with everything that moves through your mind.

Sit With This Thought

• Who's really behind the thoughts that say "you should," "you will," or "you must"?

• Have you ever acted on a thought, only to realize later it wasn't really you?

• What happens in your spirit when you choose stillness over reaction?

Try This Within

The "I" Test:

"The Journey Inward Begins with Silence"

When a thought arises, ask:

• Does it say "I" or "you"?

• Is it inviting or commanding?

• Is it peaceful or persuasive?

Label the voice. And decide who gets to speak inside you.

Stillness Activation (7 Minutes):

Close your eyes. Focus on your breath. When thoughts arise, don't follow.

Let them pass like clouds.

Breathe.

Feel the sensation in your body—from your head to your feet.

That's your soul… praying.

"The Journey Inward Begins with Silence"

CHAPTER FIVE

Knock Before You Enter

<u>The Seeking</u>

There's a difference between feeling anger… and becoming it.

Sometimes the enemy doesn't kick the door in.

He knocks.

He waits.

And then he uses your pain as the key.

"The Journey Inward Begins with Silence"

The moment your body tightens, your vision blurs, your breath shortens—he's near.

Not to take your life… but to use it.

Trauma becomes the invitation.

Unhealed wounds become the doorway.

And judgment… becomes the house we live in without realizing we were born there.

The Mirror

Knockin on Your Front Door

I almost lost it.

"The Journey Inward Begins with Silence"

He was about to overtake me—push me into something I'd regret. The rage that hit me wasn't natural. My vision blurred. My breath turned into shallow gasps like a panic attack coming on. But it wasn't just panic.

It was power.

A violent, unnatural kind of power.

Thoughts rushed into my mind that weren't mine.

He can use people—their tone, their words, even their timing—to provoke the right emotion at the wrong time. Like magic. Like a spell. A setup.

I realized something in the middle of that storm:

They call people like me narcissists.

"The Journey Inward Begins with Silence"

And maybe I got the traits. Maybe I mirror what I saw as a child.

One parent wrapped in domestic violence.

The other... a fist. Over and over.

For spilled juice. For minor toddler mistakes.

I never saw love.

Not clearly. Not purely.

Because I was blinded by what I felt instead.

That's how the devil shows up.

Not through chaos—but derealization.

That moment when you can't tell if what's happening is real, or if you're just broken.

"The Journey Inward Begins with Silence"

That's when the trauma kicks in. That's when the voice appears.

I remember the first time I heard it. I was three.

It spoke like it had always been there. It made me feel good. It made me feel bad.

It comforted me. It confused me.

And worst of all—it convinced me it was me.

Now, when I reflect...

I see the scenes like movies.

A reel of childhood pain—me in those rooms, in those moments.

And even now, the emotion doesn't fade. It tightens.

Like a hand still knockin...

"The Journey Inward Begins with Silence"

Still tryin to get in.

The Guide

Judge or Discern

You can't love what you fear.

And you can't grow past what you weren't taught.

They say nobody's perfect. But who's "they"?

According to God, we can be. Not flawless—but faithful.

Following Him isn't something you try. It becomes who you are.

Like breathing. Like blinking. You don't do it to prove anything—you do it because it's life.

"The Journey Inward Begins with Silence"

I can't say I'm a Christian yet. But I'm on my way.

I've got sins I'm working through. But I've got faith, too.

And faith means I don't get beat by what lives in my head.

I've learned people confuse discernment with judgment.

They think seeing something and reacting means you know it.

But discernment?

Discernment is quiet. It waits. It watches.

Judgment assumes.

Discernment confirms.

"The Journey Inward Begins with Silence"

I remember a moment that taught me that as a kid.

My dad made cereal for me, my brother, and my sister. But the milk was spoiled. We didn't have the words to say that. So we said it was "nasty."

He didn't believe us. He got mad. Said we were wasting food. Threatened to beat us.

We were terrified.

So we ate it anyway.

My brother got sick, ran to the bathroom throwing up.

Only after that... did my dad taste it himself.

Only then did discernment finally show up.

But by then, the damage had already been done.

"The Journey Inward Begins with Silence"

The fear had already rooted itself in our bodies.

He judged us before he understood us.

And how many of us are still doing that—to others?

To ourselves?

Sit With This Thought

• Do you know what triggers your rage—or are you afraid to look at it?

• Can you tell the difference between a thought that knocks and one that kicks the door in?

• Are you judging the pain in others… or discerning it?

Try This Within

"The Journey Inward Begins with Silence"

Check the Knock:

Next time a strong emotion rises, pause. Ask yourself:

• Who sent this?

• What does it want me to do?

• Is this mine—or just using me?

Write the answers. Don't judge. Just discern.

Disarm the Room (Memory Rewrite):

Go back to a childhood memory that still makes your body tense.

Now imagine the adult version of you stepping into that room.

What would you say to that child version of you?

"The Journey Inward Begins with Silence"

Write it out. Then say it aloud.

You are not what happened to you.

CHAPTER SIX

Where the Darkness Lives

<u>The Seeking</u>

You don't become dark overnight.

The shadows form early—in silence, in confusion, in fear too big for a child to name.

"The Journey Inward Begins with Silence"

And if they stay unchecked, they grow. Not louder, but deeper. They become part of the lens you see everything through.

What if the way you speak, the way you love, the way you leave... isn't really you?

What if it's who raised you?

What hit you?

What ignored you?

Not all scars are physical.

Some just make you flinch in ways others can't see.

The Mirror

"The Journey Inward Begins with Silence"

Internal Darkness

All actions start from within.

But not every action should come with feeling.

Sometimes emotion only makes the poison stronger.

There's this memory I can't shake.

I was no older than three. I saw myself lying on my dad's bed at his grandmother's house. I had just gotten in trouble. I can't remember if it was his fist or a belt, but I remember my eyes—trying not to cry. Trying to be strong. But scared.

I remember thinking, One day, I'm gonna have to face him.

That moment planted something.

Not just fear—doubt.

"The Journey Inward Begins with Silence"

And that doubt still tries to undo me.

My thoughts twist in on themselves.

They make me question what I said, why I did it, if I'm right for feeling what I feel.

But I'm learning: standing firm in your words makes you morally strong.

You can't backpedal every time someone else doesn't see what you see.

And hate?

Hate turns you into the very thing you're trying to avoid.

Hate your father—you become him.

Hate your mother—you take on her weight.

"The Journey Inward Begins with Silence"

So instead of hating them, I'm starting to look through them.

Most people don't even recognize the trauma that made them who they are.

When you reflect their darkness back to them, they attack—or they play victim.

But they don't see it. They can't. They won't.

That's why forgiveness isn't for them.

It's for you.

Ask God to help you forgive the ones who built your trauma… and He will.

And just like that, He'll start rebuilding you.

"The Journey Inward Begins with Silence"

<u>The Guide</u>

Issue of Trust

It's hard to trust what you don't understand.

And even harder to love what you don't feel safe around.

I've learned something:

If you can't say anything positive about someone, it's not always because they're bad—it's because something in them touches something unresolved in you.

Old wounds.

Old betrayals.

"The Journey Inward Begins with Silence"

Old standards from other people who failed you.

I pick up habits quick. Energy transfers easy. That's why I can't let everyone in.

I've noticed… I struggle to trust anyone I'm close to.

Not because they always give me a reason—but because I can't see anything good in them.

And if I can't see what's good, I assume the worst.

I start questioning:

Who's driving them?

What are they thinking?

Even if they're not doing anything… what if they could?

It's not just suspicion. It's survival.

"The Journey Inward Begins with Silence"

Even the words I love you don't sit right with me.

When someone says it constantly, it feels like reassurance for them, not expression for me.

Like they're hoping I'll say it back so they can feel secure—not because it's truth.

If your actions don't reflect your words, I can't believe them.

And if they do… then you don't have to repeat them. Once is enough.

For me, love isn't about ownership.

If I'm my own person and you're yours—this isn't a romantic trap. It's a partnership.

We don't work for each other. We work with each other.

"The Journey Inward Begins with Silence"

And real trust?

That's when your actions and your words start speaking the same language.

<u>Sit With This Thought</u>

• What memory from your childhood shaped how you love—or don't love—today?

• Have you ever hated someone so much you became like them?

• Can you name what makes you not trust others—or is it still buried?

<u>Try This Within</u>

"The Journey Inward Begins with Silence"

Shadow Spotting:

Write down the traits you hate in others.

Now ask: Have I seen these traits in someone I loved—or feared?

Then ask: Have I ever done the same?

No judgment. Just truth.

"I Love You" Inventory:

Think about the last time someone said I love you.

• Did their actions prove it?

• Did you believe them?

• Did you need them to say it—or did you just need them to show it?

Write your answer.

"The Journey Inward Begins with Silence"

Then write the version of love you believe God wants for you.

Let that be the new standard.

CHAPTER SEVEN

The Hallway Between Here and Heaven

<u>The Seeking</u>

What happens when you die?

Not the casket. Not the funeral. Not the physical ending.

But the moment right after—the silence, the space, the replay.

"The Journey Inward Begins with Silence"

What if death isn't the end of life… but the start of understanding it?

What if your soul has to walk through every moment you ever lived—one by one—until you finally see where you were wrong, who you hurt, and what you couldn't forgive?

Maybe judgment isn't God screaming at you from above.

Maybe it's you… finally seeing yourself clearly.

The Mirror

Dark Hallways

I had a thought—maybe a vision.

"The Journey Inward Begins with Silence"

When you die, maybe you don't go straight to heaven or hell.

Maybe first, you walk through a long, dark hallway.

At the end of it is a bright white light.

But the hallway isn't just darkness—it's you.

Every step along the walls is a different moment from your life.

At the very beginning: your birth.

And from there—step by step—your entire life plays out.

All the good.

All the bad.

"The Journey Inward Begins with Silence"

Every time you hurt someone.

Every time you healed someone.

Every lie. Every truth. Every choice.

But here's the twist:

You can't move forward to the next moment until you fully understand why you were wrong in the moment you're standing in.

You're stuck in that memory until you recognize what you did, who it affected, and why it mattered.

Once you see it for what it really was—you move on.

Then it happens again. And again. And again… until you reach the end of your life.

"The Journey Inward Begins with Silence"

Only then, when you've walked through all of it…

Only then can you enter the light.

I believe that's what repentance really is.

It's not just saying sorry.

It's understanding your wrong.

And if you can't see where you were wrong—you stay stuck in that part of your soul.

That's why forgiveness is so powerful.

That's why change is spiritual.

You don't go to heaven just because you die.

"The Journey Inward Begins with Silence"

You go because you let go of what kept you from being whole.

Maybe this hallway exists because God wants you to walk through yourself before you ever walk into His presence.

The Guide

Deep Truths

Emotions are reactions.

But silence is love.

Because silence means acceptance. Stillness. Peace.

Don't let your emotions bleed out for others to feed on.

"The Journey Inward Begins with Silence"

That turns inner pain into war—and emotional wars always end in destruction.

What you feel may be justified.

But how you act is not.

Lately, I've been thinking about simple things—like waking up.

We go to sleep every night.

But we don't choose to wake up.

We go through cycles—REM, deep sleep, stages we barely understand.

And somehow, without doing anything... we wake.

"The Journey Inward Begins with Silence"

That alone tells me: we're not in full control.

If we were, there'd be no such thing as comas.

No sleep paralysis. No disorders.

Waking up is grace.

So when I think about life and death—I stop trying to know it all.

We walk around trying to be somebody.

Trying to chase success. Trying to look a certain way, post the right things, say the right words.

But deep down... most people don't even know who they really are.

They've never looked.

"The Journey Inward Begins with Silence"

We're all blind to some truth about ourselves.

And the best thing we can do is experience life instead of pretending to control it.

Because when we die—honestly?

Nobody knows what happens.

That's why I believe in God.

Not because I know everything.

But because I don't.

I don't know what's waiting.

But I have faith that it's either love… or something I don't want to face unprepared.

"The Journey Inward Begins with Silence"

Sit With This Thought

• What moment from your life would keep you stuck in the hallway?

• Do you know the difference between saying sorry… and truly seeing your wrong?

• What if God doesn't have to punish you—because seeing yourself fully is the punishment?

Try This Within

The Hallway Visualization (10 Minutes):

Close your eyes. Picture a long dark hallway.

Imagine each moment of your life on the walls.

Now stop at one you regret.

"The Journey Inward Begins with Silence"

• What did you do?

• Why did you do it?

• Who did it hurt?

Ask God to help you see it clearly.

Then whisper: I forgive. I understand. I release.

Truth Over Emotion:

Next time you're overwhelmed by a feeling—pause.

Say to yourself: My emotions are not my identity.

Ask: What's true right now? What's just reaction?

Then move from truth—not reaction.

CHAPTER EIGHT

"The Journey Inward Begins with Silence"

The Eyes That Watch You

The Seeking

Sometimes you don't wake up until you see yourself in someone else.

That someone might be your child.

Their habits. Their fears. Their silence.

They reflect the parts of you you never meant to teach—but passed down anyway.

What if the things you ignore... are growing roots in someone who's watching you?

"The Journey Inward Begins with Silence"

<u>The Mirror</u>

Oblivious to Life

I had this thought.

And honestly… it made too much sense.

I'd rather walk a path with no bumps, no forks, no sudden turns.

Just one straight way.

One clear ending.

Because when there are too many options, too many intersections, too many exits…

"The Journey Inward Begins with Silence"

there's too much confusion.

Too many distractions.

Too many ways to fall off course.

Give me one direction—even if I don't know where it leads.

Because at least I'll know I'm going somewhere.

Someone once told me:

If you want to know who you are, look at your children.

Because they don't become what you say.

They become what they see.

It feels good now, seeing the world with clarity.

"The Journey Inward Begins with Silence"

I'm no longer blinded by feelings.

I can see people for who they are, not who I wish they'd be.

But even still, we can be blind to what's right in front of us when we start trusting the thoughts in our head more than the truth before our eyes.

Children don't even know what they feel.

They don't realize they're forming habits, patterns, beliefs— just from what they're soaking in.

They just exist.

But in that existence… seeds are being planted. Constantly.

Sometimes, even the healthiest-looking things become harmful—because they hide the hurt underneath.

"The Journey Inward Begins with Silence"

I prayed today.

And while I was praying, my son kept trying to get my attention.

Was it a sign from God?

Or did he just miss me enough to need my presence while I talked to the Lord?

The moment I stopped praying, he left and went back to his room.

That felt symbolic.

Like he just wanted to be near me while I was close to something divine.

"The Journey Inward Begins with Silence"

That's how I know God understands us.

It's not in the loud moments—it's in the quiet blessings.

Some miracles are obvious.

The ones you prayed for.

The ones that show up just in time.

Others are oblivious.

The ones you didn't even know you needed—until they appeared and filled a gap you couldn't name.

That's when you know it's God.

Because you couldn't have made it happen yourself.

"The Journey Inward Begins with Silence"

<u>The Guide</u>

Planted Seeds

I had a daydream.

I saw myself standing with my son.

Some guy said something disrespectful to me.

I looked at my son and said, "June Bug."

He said, "Yeah."

I said, "Get him."

And just like that, he rushed the guy and dropped him.

"The Journey Inward Begins with Silence"

Now, I know it was just a vision—just a thought.

But even in that image, I could feel his loyalty.

The kind of loyalty I still carry for my own father.

But I also realized something...

Silence is a cry for help.

Kids don't always scream.

They don't always act out.

Sometimes, they get quiet.

Because that's the only safe way they know to ask for help.

"The Journey Inward Begins with Silence"

Children don't understand emotions like we do.

And when they're overwhelmed, they're not lying—they're lost.

A kid might say they hate their parents in a moment of frustration.

But that doesn't mean they really do.

You'll know the difference—because the real ones always come back.

They soften. They hug you. They move on.

But if a child says they hate you over and over, something deeper is going on.

They might not even know why.

"The Journey Inward Begins with Silence"

And that's why punishment can't be the default.

Because if they don't understand their behavior… how can they learn from it?

Discipline without understanding is just trauma in a louder voice.

Instead, we have to teach.

We have to talk.

Not just about what they did—but about why they felt it.

And what it might mean.

Because once a child becomes traumatized…

"The Journey Inward Begins with Silence"

You can't reach them again until they know the difference between right and wrong.

And that takes patience.

Presence.

And healing you—so you don't pass your pain into their silence.

Sit With This Thought

• What have your children or younger family members unknowingly taught you about yourself?

• Do you recognize the silent signs of help in someone you love?

• Are you raising them from a place of awareness—or reaction?

Try This Within

"The Journey Inward Begins with Silence"

Break the Pattern (Reflection Drill):

Write down a phrase or habit you inherited from your parents.

Then write how it shows up in how you treat your child or others.

Ask yourself: Do I want to keep passing this on?

If not—pause, breathe, and create a new phrase.

Presence Over Punishment:

Next time a child or loved one acts out—don't react.

Ask: "What were you feeling when that happened?"

Help them name the emotion.

Let your response be a lesson—not a scar.

"The Journey Inward Begins with Silence"

CHAPTER NINE

The Scars That Spoke First

The Seeking

What if the pain wasn't meant to destroy you—but to reveal something holy inside you?

We don't just carry memories.

We carry the lessons they never gave us.

The voices we never got to use.

And the fear that taught us to obey before we ever learned to think.

"The Journey Inward Begins with Silence"

But God doesn't just speak through peace.

He speaks through realization—and some of that comes through pain.

The Mirror

History Memorials

I remember this dream from when I was a kid.

My dad woke me up by punching me—just like he'd done before.

But in the dream, he walked me to the bathroom and told me to pee.

That's when I realized… I was wetting the bed in real life.

"The Journey Inward Begins with Silence"

When I woke up and saw it, I froze.

Fear hit me instantly.

I already knew what was coming.

My dad didn't have patience.

And I didn't have protection.

Even before his fists came down, I felt the pain.

Because the memory of it was already alive in me.

And after the hitting stopped, it never really stopped.

He made me clean the room by hand.

No supplies. No tools.

"The Journey Inward Begins with Silence"

Just my hands and whatever scraps of cloth were lying around.

I dusted with old clothes.

Picked up every speck from the floor like I was the vacuum.

Put it all in a plastic trash bag.

And it wasn't just about the cleaning.

It was about control.

When I was with my mom, I could be a kid.

Watch TV. Play video games. Just exist.

But at my dad's house, those things weren't allowed.

"The Journey Inward Begins with Silence"

I remember one morning, I woke up and started watching a show.

Hadn't even gotten out of bed yet.

He came storming in, yelling.

"Why haven't you brushed your teeth?"

"Why didn't you shower?"

"Why are you just lying there?"

Six questions.

No answers.

Just fists.

"The Journey Inward Begins with Silence"

After that, he told me to clean up, then go outside.

And stay out until the streetlights came on.

I was seven years old.

That wasn't discipline.

That was trauma dressed in routine.

And what I learned—without even realizing it—was that silence keeps you safe.

That fear is easier to survive than speaking up.

"The Journey Inward Begins with Silence"

<u>The Guide</u>

Hidden Messages

When I think about death—especially children dying—it hits different now.

I don't just feel sadness.

I feel... a joyful sadness.

Because part of me knows:

Death means peace.

It means freedom from pain, stress, emotions that crash like waves.

"The Journey Inward Begins with Silence"

It means no more living under the rule of a sinful family.

No more abuse—mental or physical.

No more corruption from a broken world.

If something is truly for you—it comes without struggle.

It fits into your life naturally.

That's how I know what's divine.

God doesn't operate in emotional chaos like Satan does.

God feels—He has compassion. Empathy.

But He doesn't react emotionally like we do.

Because if He did… we'd feel His full wrath every time we sinned.

"The Journey Inward Begins with Silence"

But He doesn't move like that.

He lets us sit in our mess until we finally realize we need Him.

That's not punishment.

That's grace.

Realizations are revelations.

Someone once asked me:

"If God is real, why does Satan have so much power?"

I told them:

He doesn't.

"The Journey Inward Begins with Silence"

Satan's power is an illusion.

A lie so good, it feels like truth.

He turned away from God and tried to become his own god.

Just like many of us do.

We start doubting.

Questioning God. Questioning good.

But never once questioning evil.

No one ever asks, "Why did Satan do this to me?"

Instead, they blame God for their pain.

"The Journey Inward Begins with Silence"

Just like Satan did.

He was cast out—and still couldn't accept that his downfall came from his own choice.

That's how people live now.

Blaming God for their suffering… while ignoring the message behind the suffering.

We get so caught up in the story…

we miss the lesson inside it.

Sit With This Thought

• What memories still live inside your body—even when you're not thinking about them?

"The Journey Inward Begins with Silence"

• What pain have you mistaken as punishment… that might've been preparation?

• Are you blaming God for something Satan manipulated?

<u>Try This Within</u>

Write the Lesson, Not the Story:

Pick one painful memory from your childhood.

Write it out. Then ask:

• What did this teach me?

• What lie did I believe because of it?

Now rewrite the lesson—not from pain, but from understanding.

Practice Emotional Discernment:

"The Journey Inward Begins with Silence"

Next time you feel overwhelmed, ask:

• Is this a reaction… or a realization?

• Am I responding to what happened—or to what I believed about it?

Let God show you the message behind the moment.

CHAPTER TEN

When Silence Speaks Louder

<u>The Seeking</u>

What if the thing you hide from others is the exact key to healing yourself?

"The Journey Inward Begins with Silence"

Sometimes our deepest wounds don't scream—they sit quietly, asking not to be touched.

But even the most buried pain still grows roots.

And eventually, if you never say it out loud… it says itself in your behavior.

Healing begins when you finally put all the cards on the table.

The Mirror

Cards on the Table

I think too much.

And not in a way that makes me wise.

In a way that makes me lost.

"The Journey Inward Begins with Silence"

Some days I don't even know what I'm feeling.

It's like every emotion in me is trying to talk over the next one.

I've come a little closer to God—but I'm still searching.

When people ask if I believe, I say "no" or "I'm not sure."

But in my head?

I'm always praising Him.

The truth is—I don't really know who I am.

I only know what I can see through my own eyes.

Self-awareness is all I trust.

Everything else? Just noise.

"The Journey Inward Begins with Silence"

That uncertainty—it shapes my character without me realizing.

Makes me distant. Isolated.

But when I'm alone, my mind is clearer.

And I like that.

Still, I wish I had someone who gets me.

Someone who understands the way I move.

Someone who can sit with me in silence—and know that it means more than words.

I know only I can make myself happy.

But knowing where to start… that's the hard part.

I like being alone.

"The Journey Inward Begins with Silence"

But I also dream about having a woman who just loves me—cares for me, nurtures me, holds me down.

I know I'm not a king.

So I can't expect to be treated like one.

But still… I wish someone would cook for me. Clean for me. Take care of me in ways I've never had.

I don't expect it—but I want it.

There's a difference.

I write these things because I can't say them.

Maybe because I know expressing feelings sounds like a request for change.

And I don't want to change anyone.

"The Journey Inward Begins with Silence"

Because I wouldn't want someone trying to change me.

That's probably why I don't bring up how I feel.

It stays inside. Builds up.

I used to be happy when I worked out. When I smoked.

When my woman was all over me.

That attention—even if it seemed like I didn't want it—made me feel wanted.

I think I need that first… before I can give it back.

If you show me love, you unlock love in me.

But if you withhold it, I shut down.

I stay quiet because that's what I learned.

"The Journey Inward Begins with Silence"

As a kid, I had to absorb so much without ever speaking on it.

Now I carry it like weight—on my back, in my stomach, in my silence.

I don't need people.

But I'd love to have someone beside me.

Someone who doesn't fix me—but grows with me.

I remember being punished for speaking my mind.

That was traumatic.

They told me to speak—but when I said something they didn't like, I got punished.

That's how silence becomes safer than honesty.

"The Journey Inward Begins with Silence"

And now…

That's how I live.

The Guide

Casual Norm

I'm working on overcoming all this.

I'm trying.

But it's hard.

Whenever I'm in a relationship and we're apart, my mind
plays tricks on me.

Gives me images—her with someone else.

"The Journey Inward Begins with Silence"

Her leaving.

Her not loving me like I love her.

It makes me anxious.

Makes me jealous.

And even though I don't act on it… I feel it.

And when you care about someone, that fear of being hurt starts messing with your trust.

I feel it in my stomach first.

That tight emotion.

But I hold it. I don't let it speak.

"The Journey Inward Begins with Silence"

Writing helps.

I never know when something I write is going to hit.

Sometimes the message reveals itself in seconds.

Sometimes it takes months.

But it always says something back.

Throughout the day, I'll get flashes—faces.

No words. Just a flicker of someone's image and a wave of anxiety in my gut.

Like there's something unresolved between us.

To most people, those feelings go unnoticed.

But for me?

They don't go away.

"The Journey Inward Begins with Silence"

It's like emotional pop-ups on a computer.

Sudden. Loud. Distracting.

Most people don't notice until the moment after—when they're apologizing for something they couldn't explain.

But I live in it.

And honestly?

It feels like hell sometimes.

So I wonder…

Was it me?

"The Journey Inward Begins with Silence"

Did I do something to deserve this pain?

Or was it your mind that convinced you to treat me a certain way—based on how you felt?

That's what makes healing hard.

When you can't trust your thoughts.

When your emotions lie.

And when your silence becomes the only thing that still feels safe.

Sit With This Thought

• Do you shut down or speak up when something hurts you?

• How did your childhood teach you to handle feelings—by voice or by silence?

"The Journey Inward Begins with Silence"

• Are you waiting for someone to understand you… before you allow yourself to be seen?

<u>Try This Within</u>

Write What You Can't Say:

Take 10 minutes. No filter.

Write down the feelings you've never spoken—especially the ones you thought would scare people away.

Then read them back.

Would you ever judge someone else for feeling this way?

Emotional Triggers Map:

Keep track of when you feel tension in your stomach or chest.

What were you thinking about? Who did you see?

"The Journey Inward Begins with Silence"

Label the trigger—but don't act.

Breathe. Reflect.

Let understanding replace the emotional reflex.

CHAPTER ELEVEN

Mind Games & Soul Ties

The Seeking

Sometimes it's not the person that traps you. It's the thought that you need them.

Relationships are spiritual mirrors.

"The Journey Inward Begins with Silence"

They show us where we heal… and where we still hide.

But love without growth is just attachment.

And attachment without truth is a trap.

The real relationship starts when you stop lying to yourself about what you want—and why you stay.

The Mirror

Relationship Tricks

Every day is a chance to learn something new.

Not just about the world—but about yourself.

"The Journey Inward Begins with Silence"

And when you're open to those lessons, life starts moving differently.

Being around my son and his mom, I notice how uncomfortable he seems sometimes.

And even though me and his mother are cool—we're not friends.

Not in the real way.

We co-exist. That's it.

I found out she has a boyfriend now.

And honestly—I'm happy for her.

But my mind still tried to make me jealous.

Even though I got someone waiting for me at home.

"The Journey Inward Begins with Silence"

That's how I know the mind is a trickster.

It plays games you never agreed to play.

Just hearing her talk about relationships, I could tell she still moves selfishly.

She doesn't date for the right reasons.

But that's her road to walk—her lesson to learn.

I also talked to someone else recently.

Someone who seems to regret not giving us a real shot.

She's in a relationship now.

But she's not happy.

She sees how selfish her partner is...

But she stays.

"The Journey Inward Begins with Silence"

Not because she loves him.

But because she's scared to be alone.

And that's what I'm seeing everywhere now—

People staying in relationships just to avoid silence.

Just to avoid their own company.

A woman could be getting abused every day and still won't leave.

Not because she can't…

But because her mind convinced her she has to stay.

It's the mind.

That's the real prison.

"The Journey Inward Begins with Silence"

Because unless you're cuffed to a wall, you're free.

But if your mind says you're stuck—you believe it.

You should never be with someone for what they have or what they can do for you.

That's not love.

That's survival.

The only true reason men and women should come together?

To learn from each other.

And maybe, to create life.

Everything else?

"The Journey Inward Begins with Silence"

That's just distraction in disguise.

<u>The Guide</u>

Questions to Them

Here's the mind-fuck of the day:

We live on a round Earth, right?

Then what's really up… and what's down?

If the planet spins, does that mean someone, somewhere is literally standing upside down looking into space?

Who made up laws?

"The Journey Inward Begins with Silence"

Who decided what was right or wrong—and when?

When do you know it's wrong to kill someone?

And if we claim to know God—how do we know Him?

What does He sound like?

Does He answer through signs?

Through thoughts?

Through dreams?

Through silence?

And what if He never answers at all?

Then what?

"The Journey Inward Begins with Silence"

Do you know your own purpose?

Do you even know yourself?

How do you control emotion?

Is emotion a cause?

Or is it a reaction?

Can you start an emotion… without a reason?

Some days I sit back and wonder:

How will it all end for me?

Is worrying about myself a sin?

"The Journey Inward Begins with Silence"

Or is it survival?

If I could ask God for one thing—

It wouldn't be money.

It wouldn't be fame.

It would be this:

Eternal peace.

Sit With This Thought

• Have you ever stayed in a relationship to avoid being alone?

• Is your love rooted in truth—or fear?

"The Journey Inward Begins with Silence"

• Are your questions about God keeping you from hearing Him?

Try This Within

Emotional Exit Drill:

Think of one situation or person you stayed connected to— even though it made you uncomfortable.

Ask yourself:

• What fear kept me there?

• What story did my mind tell me?

• What would I gain by letting go?

Ask Without Expecting:

"The Journey Inward Begins with Silence"

Write down three deep questions you've always had about life or God.

Don't answer them.

Just write them.

Then sit in stillness and let your spirit begin to answer slowly, over time, through signs, feelings, or silence.

CHAPTER TWELVE

The Thought About the Thought

The Seeking

"The Journey Inward Begins with Silence"

Not every thought belongs to you. Some just visit to see if you'll feed them.

The mind is a noisy room.

And Satan doesn't knock—he whispers.

Learning to doubt your thoughts doesn't make you weak.

It makes you free.

Because the moment you believe every thought is you…

you become whatever your mind tells you.

The Mirror

Thought of Doubting Thoughts

"The Journey Inward Begins with Silence"

I'm learning to doubt every thought.

Not just the dark ones.

But even the ones that sound like truth.

Because Satan knows when to show up.

Right when your spirit is vulnerable.

Right when you're in your most silent spaces—he whispers the loudest.

I think back to my past—when nothing worked in my favor.

When I felt like the whole world was pushing against me.

But now, things have shifted.

"The Journey Inward Begins with Silence"

I don't feel in need anymore.

I feel needed.

I don't crave love—I'm wanted.

That's what happens when you face reality:

You see every moment as a choice.

Right or wrong.

Not based on what benefits you—but on truth.

Sometimes the right choice doesn't reward you.

And the wrong choice gives you instant comfort.

But it's still a choice.

"The Journey Inward Begins with Silence"

I notice it in people too.

How their attitude shifts—even when they don't mean for it to.

They respond vaguely. Give you the silent treatment.

Their spirit starts showing—without saying a word.

That's how I know the spirit in them isn't at peace.

So I don't judge it.

I have compassion for it.

Because when someone's mind is filled with chaotic thoughts…

that's when Satan is working overtime.

"The Journey Inward Begins with Silence"

He doesn't always come through anger.

Sometimes he comes through silence.

Through isolation.

Through that slow transition from joy to numbness.

When your attitude changes from open to closed…

That's when you know he's pulling you in.

Doubt every thought the moment it comes.

A thought about someone else shouldn't change your mood.

A thought about yourself shouldn't steal your peace.

Even the thought of thinking…

"The Journey Inward Begins with Silence"

deserves doubt.

Because on our own, we can do nothing.

Only through God does clarity come.

The Guide

The Thought to See

I don't need to be right.

But I want to make sense.

I want the most realistic answer for any situation.

Not the answer that makes me look good.

"The Journey Inward Begins with Silence"

But the one that fits both sides.

I try not to judge what I see.

I just call it what it is.

A cow without horns? Not a bull.

A man with male biology? Not a woman.

It's not hate.

It's just clarity.

When I listen to people speak, I can hear their tone change.

They don't want truth.

They want agreement.

"The Journey Inward Begins with Silence"

They want confirmation that what they believe is right.

Disagreements feel like attacks now.

Nobody wants to be challenged.

They've become so identified with their thoughts…

that disagreeing with their opinion feels like a threat to their identity.

And for a long time, I didn't think I could be wrong either.

If I didn't know something, I figured it could be learned—or someone had the answer.

But now, I see that even my thoughts…

are deeper than I can sometimes understand.

"The Journey Inward Begins with Silence"

Sometimes I think something—then later sit there wondering what I even meant.

Because the message didn't come from me.

It came through me.

There are messages in everything.

In people.

In moments.

In silence.

But you won't see them until you're ready.

And when you are—change begins.

Don't be thankful for the change.

"The Journey Inward Begins with Silence"

Be thankful for the sight.

Because without seeing, change wouldn't even be possible.

And you'd still be sitting in your head...

wondering what it means

to think the thoughts

you thought you thought.

Sit With This Thought

• What thoughts have you believed that weren't even yours?

• Do you respond to thoughts as if they are commands—or whispers to examine?

• What if seeing clearly was more important than always being right?

"The Journey Inward Begins with Silence"

<u>Try This Within</u>

Doubt It On Arrival:

When a strong thought or emotion hits—pause and ask:

• Who does this serve?

• Is this from me, my pain, or something darker?

Then breathe. Detach. Respond only if it aligns with peace.

Message Decoding Exercise:

Write a deep thought you've had lately that left you wondering what it meant.

Re-read it tomorrow.

Ask God to show you the meaning through life, not logic.

Be still enough to see when it shows up.

CHAPTER THIRTEEN

The Moment You Wake Up

<u>The Seeking</u>

Truth doesn't enter your life through facts—it enters through experience.

Spiritual birth doesn't happen in church.

It doesn't come with a sermon or a scripture.

It happens the moment you start questioning the world…

and the self…

"The Journey Inward Begins with Silence"

and everything you thought you were.

Because when the spirit wakes up—

it doesn't whisper.

It shakes your whole identity.

The Mirror

Birth of the Spirit

I was raised to keep feelings to myself.

To hold them in.

To never speak unless spoken to.

To stay silent even when I was hurting.

"The Journey Inward Begins with Silence"

That silence became survival.

But it also caused something I couldn't explain as a kid—

a derealization.

I remember asking my mom,

"Am I dreaming? Is this real?"

Because nothing felt real.

It was like watching my life from the outside, in.

I didn't understand it then—

but I was waking up too early to things that should've been taught with love.

"The Journey Inward Begins with Silence"

Now, as an adult, I feel the shift.

I can see emotions before they come.

I can sense when a thought doesn't belong to me.

And I feel like I have choices now—

real ones.

Some things aren't learned.

They're revealed.

In one moment, you see something clearly...

and you never see the same way again.

That's not education.

That's revelation.

"The Journey Inward Begins with Silence"

Thinking about the answer isn't the same as receiving one.

And most of the time—

our thoughts aren't even ours.

Can you explain how a thought is created?

Step-by-step?

Can you explain where emotions begin?

We think we know.

But most of what we "know" is just what we were told.

Passed down. Repeated. Reinforced.

But real truth?

"The Journey Inward Begins with Silence"

It reveals itself.

And when it does, it changes you instantly.

You don't have to force it.

You don't have to memorize it.

It shows up and applies itself to your life right there, on the spot.

Once you start questioning what you've always believed—

you find out...

you were raised in lies.

The Guide

Brain Works

"The Journey Inward Begins with Silence"

What I know—

and what I think I know—

has me in constant deep thought.

But I'm starting to realize…

I'm not in control of any of it.

I'm just a passenger.

Watching this world.

Taking it in.

I try not to talk in my head.

But it happens unconsciously.

"The Journey Inward Begins with Silence"

Sometimes I notice the thoughts.

They run on loop.

And when I become aware of them—

they stop.

But then… I start responding.

Still in my head.

Still trapped in dialogue I didn't start.

I wish I could write all of it down.

But these thoughts come randomly.

All throughout the day.

"The Journey Inward Begins with Silence"

Still, I know one thing now:

My thoughts are real.

Not "true"—but real.

They affect me.

They shape my lens.

I looked at the Bible recently…

And I noticed—most scriptures are written in either first or third person.

Almost like they were coming from someone's mind.

From someone's heart.

"The Journey Inward Begins with Silence"

Someone like me.

I read it…

And I saw myself in it.

Not the same message.

But the same spirit.

It made me question even more:

Where in scripture does it say God created planets?

I couldn't find it.

So what if… we're not even on one?

"The Journey Inward Begins with Silence"

I know for sure this, though—

Marriage was never about love or happiness.

It was about stability.

About raising children in unity.

About keeping the parents together for their upbringing.

And if there are no kids—

maybe…

there is no reason for marriage.

Sit With This Thought

"The Journey Inward Begins with Silence"

• What are some truths that revealed themselves to you—not through learning, but through experience?

• Are your beliefs based on what was passed down to you… or what has been revealed to you?

• What if you're not here to discover truth—but to remember it?

<u>Try This Within</u>

Write the Moment You Woke Up:

Describe one moment in your life where you saw through something that used to feel "normal."

What did it show you about yourself? About others? About God?

Silent Thought Tracking:

"The Journey Inward Begins with Silence"

Spend 5 minutes each morning in silence.

Notice what thoughts come up.

Don't judge them. Just ask:

• "Is this mine?"

• "Is this truth?"

• "Is this teaching me—or trapping me?"

Let your awareness be your protection.

CHAPTER FOURTEEN

The Church Was Always Inside You

<u>The Seeking</u>

"The Journey Inward Begins with Silence"

God is not hiding in a building. He's waiting in your silence.

You can go to church your whole life and never meet God.

Because God doesn't live in sermons—He lives in surrender.

In awareness. In revelation. In truth that finds you when you're finally still enough to listen.

The Mirror

Church Within

Why do people go to church?

"The Journey Inward Begins with Silence"

Is it to know God?

To wash away sins?

To become saved?

To fellowship?

I remember being a child—confused, bored, and forced to sit in a building where people sang songs and read from a book I didn't understand.

I didn't know who God was.

I didn't even know why I was there.

But I had no choice.

My mother and great-grandmother made me go.

And honestly?

"The Journey Inward Begins with Silence"

Church is no place for children.

They don't have sins to wash away.

They don't need to be "saved."

They don't even understand what life is yet, let alone God.

Forcing them into something they don't connect with only pushes them away.

It pushed me away.

Not from God.

But from the idea of God.

"The Journey Inward Begins with Silence"

Now that I'm older, I see it clearer.

You can go to church for years… and never find Him.

Because you're looking too far outside yourself.

And all along, He's been within you.

When I talk to my younger cousins, I see the same confusion I had.

One says they believe.

The other says, "Yeah, but He's just a man in the clouds."

Neither of them understands.

They just repeat what they've been told.

And yet—neither of them has even stepped foot in a church.

"The Journey Inward Begins with Silence"

But they know of God.

Because God is not a place.

He's presence.

And that presence?

Lives inside you.

The Guide

Clear Pathways

For the first time in my life—

emptiness feels good.

"The Journey Inward Begins with Silence"

And that's how I know truth has entered.

Because it didn't come with noise.

It came with peace.

The freedom I feel now…

it's not loud or dramatic.

It's quiet.

Simple.

Powerful.

I don't "think" anymore.

I just know God is with me.

"The Journey Inward Begins with Silence"

There's a new life rising in me.

I can feel it.

Maybe forgiving my father was the breath my soul needed.

Maybe that was the key that unlocked something I'd buried.

People want.

People need.

But even when they receive—they still want more.

That's how I know satisfaction doesn't come from getting.

It comes from surrender.

Tonight I prayed.

"The Journey Inward Begins with Silence"

And like always—random thoughts came.

But I didn't fear them.

I felt aware.

Present.

Not afraid.

In the middle of the noise, I saw flashes of my past writings.

Moments where I praised God for little things.

I remembered those exact moments.

And that told me—He remembered them too.

He was watching over me then.

Just like He's with me now.

"The Journey Inward Begins with Silence"

That's how I know He's real.

Because even in my silence, He speaks.

Even in my confusion, He remembers.

So now… I cherish every little thing.

Even my last breath—if that's all I'm given—will be a gift.

Sit With This Thought

• Did you learn about God through tradition—or through revelation?

• Is your connection to God internal… or inherited?

• What if silence was the only sermon you ever needed?

"The Journey Inward Begins with Silence"

Try This Within

Rebuild the Temple:

Close your eyes and imagine what God looks like inside you.

Not in a building. Not in a pulpit.

Inside your breath. Your stillness. Your forgiveness.

Ask Him to reveal Himself there.

Little Gratitudes Journal:

Start a list.

Each night, write one small thing you noticed that felt like God's presence.

A moment. A memory. A peace that didn't make sense.

"The Journey Inward Begins with Silence"

Watch how your awareness builds the real church—within.

CHAPTER FIFTEEN

From the Mind to the Spirit

The Seeking

You can't live outwardly free while thinking inwardly broken.

When the mind is bruised, the body follows.

When the spirit heals, the mind obeys.

"The Journey Inward Begins with Silence"

There's no transformation without truth.

No peace without surrender.

No love without renewal.

The Mirror

Mental Bruising Physical

I'm starting this one off the only way I know how:

I love you, God.

I want to see myself for who I really am.

And I want to help others see the same.

"The Journey Inward Begins with Silence"

Keep working on me.

Make me more like you.

Walk me into your image—one truth at a time.

Deliver me from every evil, every lie, every temptation Satan and his children might bring.

Bless me with your spiritual wisdom.

Your divine love.

So I can carry light into this world—into all its dark places.

I don't wish harm on anybody.

In fact, I wish health and healing for everyone on earth.

So they too can walk in your image.

"The Journey Inward Begins with Silence"

Because here's what I've learned:

The mind is a dangerous place when it isn't disciplined.

People who live inside their minds more than they live in the world?

They're disconnected.

And that imagination becomes a replacement for truth.

But imagination isn't reality.

And living in your head won't save you.

When your thoughts are misaligned with truth, they still influence your actions.

And that's why spiritual discipline is everything.

"The Journey Inward Begins with Silence"

There's always a time for everything…

but no time for wasting.

I look back on my childhood and realize:

Hate starts young.

It begins in children who are punished without purpose.

Who are bruised physically and mentally and never given explanation—only pain.

I remember as a preteen, sneaking into my grandma's house with my cousins just to use the bathroom.

We were locked out while the adults left.

None of us were older than 12.

"The Journey Inward Begins with Silence"

When they came back and caught us coming out the house, they lined us up and decided we all needed to be whipped.

We each took two strikes to the hands with a leather alligator belt.

But when it was my turn—I didn't cry.

I didn't flinch.

That was my mistake.

They took my stillness as disrespect.

Thought I wasn't learning a lesson.

So I got more.

"The Journey Inward Begins with Silence"

My step-uncle whipped my legs and ankles with force.

But still, I didn't cry.

Because it didn't hurt—not really.

It was familiar.

It was normal.

Eventually, I pretended to whine, just so it would stop.

But even then—I was only faking the pain they expected me to feel.

Because the real pain…

was already inside.

"The Journey Inward Begins with Silence"

<u>The Guide</u>

Living Inside Out

Sitting in the presence of the Lord... I feel good.

Actually—I feel great.

I've stopped asking for specifics.

Now I just say:

Let your will be done.

Because I don't know the future.

And I don't need to.

I trust the One who does.

"The Journey Inward Begins with Silence"

Whatever comes—

I'll meet it with peace.

I'll handle it the right way.

It's crazy how others look at my life and call it inspirational.

To me, it's just logic.

Normal.

Basic obedience.

And maybe that's the problem…

Maybe what's "normal" to me, is divine to someone else.

If I'm blessed with another life to raise, I'll give more.

"The Journey Inward Begins with Silence"

I'll pour double what I've been given.

Because I believe…

I believe in the Lord's name.

I believe in His blessings.

And I believe my life will reflect His glory.

I don't carry fear anymore.

There's not one thing—not one person—I fear.

No man.

No woman.

Can control me.

"The Journey Inward Begins with Silence"

I make sound decisions through the mind of the Lord.

My heart?

It's pure.

No hate left.

Only love.

Only purpose.

I don't act for reactions anymore.

I act for meaning.

Because life is not random.

There are reasons for every moment.

And moments for every reason.

"The Journey Inward Begins with Silence"

If the sun never moved…

If night never came…

There'd be no such thing as yesterday or tomorrow.

There is only now.

And what you do now shapes what comes next.

There are only two days in life:

The day you live.

And the day you die.

Everything in between…

is your choice.

"The Journey Inward Begins with Silence"

<u>Sit With This Thought</u>

• Have you been punished more than you've been heard?

• Are your reactions based on pain—or purpose?

• Are you finally ready to live inside out?

<u>Try This Within</u>

Reality Check-In:

The next time you feel triggered—pause. Ask:

• Is this pain from now or from my past?

• Am I responding to the moment or to a memory?

Write what comes up. Don't judge it. Just release it.

Living From the Spirit:

"The Journey Inward Begins with Silence"

For one full day, try this rule:

Every action must come from purpose, not reaction.

Every word must pass through love, not fear.

At the end of the day, reflect on what changed.

CHAPTER SIXTEEN

The War Is Over When You Forgive

<u>The Seeking</u>

What if the prison you're trying to escape is built from the grudges you won't release?

"The Journey Inward Begins with Silence"

You can't walk into your higher self while carrying lower emotions.

Forgiveness isn't about forgetting what happened—it's about remembering who you are beyond it.

The Mirror

Forgiveness Pt. 2

There comes a moment in your life where you stop being the main character—and start being the foundation.

That moment comes when someone depends on you. A child. A partner. Even your own reflection.

"The Journey Inward Begins with Silence"

And when they do… your life stops being about what happened to you—and starts being about what you'll do with it.

I met my father when I was three years old.

And I forgave him when I was twenty-three.

Two decades between encounter and healing.

Two decades of carrying pain I didn't create, but inherited.

He wasn't raised to be a father.

He and his brother raised themselves.

So his idea of discipline wasn't built on love—it was built on survival.

"The Journey Inward Begins with Silence"

I remember him telling me, "I used to sock you because you weren't tough."

But I was never meant to be tough.

I was just trying to be seen. Heard. Understood.

That's the difference between strength and armor.

One is rooted in identity. The other? Trauma.

Still… as much as I thought forgiveness would feel like tearing open a wound—it felt more like releasing something that was never mine to hold.

There were no fireworks.

No breakdowns.

No long speeches.

"The Journey Inward Begins with Silence"

Just a moment.

A man.

And a choice.

And when I made that choice, I saw him—not as the monster from my memories, but as a man trying to explain his own.

I realized that most of our suffering doesn't come from the event itself...

It comes from the stories we rehearse about the event, over and over in our minds.

Forgiveness isn't hard.

Thinking about forgiveness is.

"The Journey Inward Begins with Silence"

Because thought will lie to you.

It will whisper that forgiveness is betrayal.

That letting go is weakness.

That they don't deserve it.

But forgiveness has never been about them.

It's about you.

And when I let go, I was reborn.

And I felt it—that quiet miracle.

My relationship with both of my parents—though scarred—
was still a gift.

"The Journey Inward Begins with Silence"

Still better than the hand they were dealt.

And now, through me, the story is changing.

The Guide

Good vs. Evil

Some nights, I try to close my eyes and find peace—

But what greets me is a version of myself I barely recognize.

The thoughts are sharp. Violent.

And the scariest part is… in those dreams, I'm the one causing the harm.

"The Journey Inward Begins with Silence"

This is the curse of consciousness.

The more aware you become, the more you see the duality in yourself.

But most people?

They think knowing of God is the same as knowing Him.

It's not.

There are only two paths in this life—

The path of good, with God.

And the path of evil, with the enemy.

"The Journey Inward Begins with Silence"

And evil? It's clever.

It doesn't show up with horns and fire.

It shows up with just enough light to pass.

Just enough "truth" to fool you.

It gives you highs, then strips you bare.

It gives you pleasure, then replaces it with chaos.

It mimics everything divine—without the divine presence.

And you think you're choosing freedom...

But you're really choosing confusion.

The truth?

"The Journey Inward Begins with Silence"

There's no such thing as free will when you're enslaved by emotion.

Good, on the other hand, doesn't need to shout.

It arrives gently.

Blessings fall in disguise.

Doors open without begging.

Needs are met before they're spoken.

You love differently on this path.

You feel compassion even for the people who tried to break you.

You can look at the face of your enemy—and see fear instead of threat.

"The Journey Inward Begins with Silence"

Because now you understand.

They don't hate you—they're scared of the light in you.

I once spoke to someone who said, "God is both good and evil."

She believed our punishment was proof of His cruelty.

But I see it differently.

God doesn't punish us.

He allows us to feel the weight of our own disobedience.

To teach.

To correct.

To awaken.

"The Journey Inward Begins with Silence"

If God was both love and hate, where would Satan even fit?

God can't contradict Himself.

He said it Himself in Scripture:

"If you hate your brother, the love of God is not in you."

How can you claim to love what you cannot see,

when you despise what's right in front of you?

That's not faith.

That's fiction.

Sit With This Thought

"The Journey Inward Begins with Silence"

• Who have you given too much power by holding on to what they did?

• Has not forgiving them really kept you safe—or just kept you stuck?

• Are you open to the idea that freedom isn't always loud, but peace is always quiet?

<u>Try This Within</u>

The Letter You'll Never Send

Write to the one who hurt you.

Pour it all out—uncensored.

Then burn it.

Let the fire consume what no longer belongs in your body.

"The Journey Inward Begins with Silence"

3-Day Forgiveness Fast

For the next three days:

• No revenge thoughts.

• No mental arguments.

• No reliving old pain.

When it rises, say aloud: "That is not mine anymore."

Watch how much lighter you become.

CHAPTER SEVENTEEN

The Realignment

The Seeking

"The Journey Inward Begins with Silence"

What if your passion was planted in you before the pain—and your healing is what unlocks it?

You can't grow into purpose while holding someone else's expectations.

Your life blooms when your identity is no longer borrowed—but revealed.

The Mirror

Light in View

I used to say I wanted to join the service.

But looking back, that was never really my dream.

It was my father's.

"The Journey Inward Begins with Silence"

He mentioned it once, and I held onto it—

Not because it made sense,

But because I wanted to make sense to him.

Truth is, my whole life I loved building things.

Legos, construction kits, drawing sets.

I was fascinated with structure.

Not just physical structures—mental ones.

Framework.

Design.

Blueprints.

Someone close to me reminded me of that recently.

"The Journey Inward Begins with Silence"

And now I see it clear…

My goals have always been there.

Waiting.

I want to buy land.

Build on it.

Create something real from my own hands and imagination.

It all goes hand-in-hand—who I was, who I am, and who I'm becoming.

That's the thing about purpose.

It doesn't shout.

It whispers.

"The Journey Inward Begins with Silence"

Softly. Consistently.

Until you stop chasing noise and start listening to silence.

I thought I needed something big to find God again.

But all He asked me for… was forgiveness.

Forgiveness for my mother.

Not in thought—but in person.

And the moment I said I would,

she called to say she was coming over.

That's not coincidence.

That's divine alignment.

"The Journey Inward Begins with Silence"

God speaks through every interaction.

Every encounter.

Every shift in atmosphere.

But you won't notice it unless your heart is open.

Now I walk in prayer.

And in this posture—I don't chase anything.

Because when you're in divine flow,

you don't need or want.

Everything is added unto you.

"The Journey Inward Begins with Silence"

<u>The Guide</u>

Learning Ways

These days, when I ask myself what my goals are…

There's only one answer that feels true:

Get closer to God.

That's it.

That's the goal.

Everything else—money, purpose, peace—flows from that.

"The Journey Inward Begins with Silence"

I was praying the other day and my mind felt clearer than it has in a long time.

And I saw something—myself, speaking to my son.

I told him, "Don't hate. I see myself in you."

And I understood the true meaning of love your neighbor as yourself—because I was looking at the younger version of me, right in front of me.

That same day, I checked my gas account.

I expected a balance… but instead found a $215 credit.

Some might call it coincidence.

"The Journey Inward Begins with Silence"

I call it a blessing in disguise.

It's the little things people overlook—

But I see God in all of them.

And lately, even my writing feels different.

Like I'm speaking from a place I never knew I had access to.

Almost like I can't fully relate to who I was in my past journal entries.

That's how I know healing is happening.

See, we don't realize how much our upbringing shapes our instincts.

"The Journey Inward Begins with Silence"

If you were punished physically for cursing as a child,

You'll probably discipline your own children the same way.

Not because you want to…

But because it's what's wired in you.

The guilt shows up later.

In the quiet.

In the reflection.

In the tears you hide when you hear your child cry.

You remember how it felt.

Not just the pain.

But the confusion.

The loneliness.

"The Journey Inward Begins with Silence"

The realization hits:

You're not just raising your child.

You're reliving your childhood.

And rewriting the parts you never healed.

Sit With This Thought

• Are you living the life you desire—or one someone else told you to want?

• Have you confused obedience with identity?

• Can you see your childhood patterns showing up in your adult relationships?

Try This Within

"The Journey Inward Begins with Silence"

Realignment Check:

List 3 things you used to love as a child.

Not things that impressed others—things that lit you up.

Ask yourself:

• How can I bring one of these back into my life this week?

Parenting the Inner Child:

When emotions rise—ask yourself:

• Is this how I would want to be treated when I felt this way as a child?

Let that answer guide how you respond to others—and to yourself.

CHAPTER EIGHTEEN

"The Journey Inward Begins with Silence"

Who's Really Guiding You?

<u>The Seeking</u>

Are you living by faith—or by force?

Sometimes we think we're in control, but life keeps asking us: Who's really steering your soul?

Until you answer that, your spirit can't truly rest.

<u>The Mirror</u>

Message to God

Patiently waiting.

"The Journey Inward Begins with Silence"

That's where I've been lately.

Not for money.

Not for success.

But for salvation.

I want to be saved.

Fully.

No halfway faith.

No second guessing.

No more questioning if He's listening—I know He is.

Because every day, something in me shifts.

And every shift brings me closer to Him.

"The Journey Inward Begins with Silence"

I see it in the way I speak now.

The way I move.

The way I respond.

There's clarity in me that didn't exist before.

Like I've been walking through fog my whole life and now the path is finally clearing.

At first, I wondered… were all these signs just coincidence?

But the more they came, the more I realized:

This ain't chance.

This is God.

I feel it.

"The Journey Inward Begins with Silence"

That warmth in my chest when I'm writing.

That calm in my body when I stop overthinking.

That overwhelming peace when I pray.

That's Him.

I can't always explain it, but I know when He's near.

And now, all I ask for is strength.

The strength to keep going.

To fight the good fight.

To share the truth—even when it feels heavy.

Even when it hurts.

I know there's a war between good and evil.

"The Journey Inward Begins with Silence"

I just want to be on the right side of it.

I don't want to just survive it.

I want to win it.

And when it's all said and done—

I want to go home.

Not to a place.

But to Him.

The Guide

Mental Guidance

I've been thinking a lot lately about baptism.

"The Journey Inward Begins with Silence"

Not the water part—

But the rebirth part.

What does it really mean to be born again?

Is it about getting dunked in water?

Or is it about letting go of your old self?

If the kingdom of God is within you,

then maybe being born again has less to do with ceremony

and more to do with repentance and forgiveness.

Letting go of the ego.

"The Journey Inward Begins with Silence"

Letting God drive.

Because whether people realize it or not,

we're all being guided by something.

Every encounter we have with someone else creates a ripple.

Sometimes it's small.

Sometimes it leaves a mark for life.

And one day, when we're in that dark hallway with God...

We'll have to walk through every moment.

Every feeling.

Every ripple.

"The Journey Inward Begins with Silence"

Not to be punished—

But to understand.

To see why we did what we did.

Why we felt how we felt.

That's real judgment.

That's divine reflection.

So I ask myself often:

Who's guiding me when I make decisions?

Is it love?

Or is it fear?

"The Journey Inward Begins with Silence"

Is it God?

Or is it the part of me still wounded?

Because I've noticed—

When my state of mind shifts from peace to chaos,

there's always a spirit behind it.

It could be someone else's energy.

It could be my own emotions.

But if I pause, recognize it, and don't react—

The negativity fades.

"The Journey Inward Begins with Silence"

It hates being seen.

It hates being exposed.

And the only thing stronger than that darkness is love.

Real love.

The kind that doesn't retaliate.

The kind that stands its ground in peace.

Love conquers all.

That's not just a saying.

That's spiritual law.

And it's the most underrated message in the world today.

"The Journey Inward Begins with Silence"

<u>Sit With This Thought</u>

• Who or what has been guiding your decisions lately?

• Are you reacting to life—or surrendering to it?

• Do you recognize the difference between your emotions and your spirit?

<u>Try This Within</u>

Spiritual GPS Check:

For one day, pause before every decision (even the small ones) and ask:

"Is this me… or something guiding me?"

Write down what comes up.

"The Journey Inward Begins with Silence"

Reactive Reset:

The next time you feel your peace shift, don't respond right away.

• Breathe.

• Ask where the emotion is coming from.

• Speak this aloud: "Peace is my path. I won't be pulled."

Watch the energy change.

CHAPTER NINETEEN

See It for What It Is

The Seeking

"The Journey Inward Begins with Silence"

Are you viewing life through clear sight—or through emotional fog?

The eyes can be perfect and still be blind.

Real vision begins when you stop letting pain narrate the story.

The Mirror

Voice from Above

People talk about free will like it's just a spiritual theory.

But the truth is—we live it every day.

You have the freedom to do whatever your mind can imagine.

And no one can truly stop you.

"The Journey Inward Begins with Silence"

But every choice comes with a consequence.

That's the part people forget.

We think our emotions give us a right to act.

But just because you feel it, doesn't mean it's right to do it.

Emotions are dangerous like that.

They're mixed personalities—temporary, shifting, unstable.

They don't always come from you.

And they don't always lead where you think they will.

That's why I've learned:

Treat people how you want to be treated.

"The Journey Inward Begins with Silence"

Even when you're mad.

Even when they don't deserve it.

Because how you treat others is a reflection of how you've trained yourself to respond.

And hate?

That's just emotional weakness wearing a mask of control.

I don't want to hate anybody.

I want to love everybody—equally.

Because when your mind is strong, your heart becomes stronger.

And when your heart is strong, your life starts producing peace.

"The Journey Inward Begins with Silence"

No one can control your outcome except you.

No one can think for you.

And no one can see what's inside you… unless you give them access.

So be cautious with your thoughts.

Be honest with your emotions.

And be generous with your love.

That's the only formula that works.

The Guide

"The Journey Inward Begins with Silence"

Twenty Twenty

I look around and see beauty.

Green trees. Blue skies.

Architectural structures that make me pause.

But I also see something else…

Blindness.

People smiling, joking, going about their day—completely unaware of the war inside themselves.

They laugh.

But they're numb.

"The Journey Inward Begins with Silence"

They enjoy life…

But they're detached from it.

I remember being a kid and wondering why my parents weren't together.

I had never even seen them in the same room as anything more than strangers.

A friend of mine once said she never felt that way—

But she also had no relationship with her father.

That hit me.

Sometimes, we confuse apologizing with forgiving.

We think saying "sorry" to our parents makes it all go away.

"The Journey Inward Begins with Silence"

But most of the time, we're not apologizing for what we did.

We're apologizing for how we responded to what they did.

Even when they're not around, we're still reacting to the imprint they left on us.

The sad truth is…

Forgiveness isn't about right or wrong.

It's about freedom.

Because the moment you hold a grudge, you give that person power over your peace.

And if the person you resent is your parent—

"The Journey Inward Begins with Silence"

Then your whole life becomes a contradiction.

You'll act out of love in some areas,

And out of hate in others—

Without even realizing you've been split in two.

You forget why you were angry in the first place.

You grow up thinking it's just "how you are."

But really...

You've just been living from a memory you stopped remembering.

The only way back?

"The Journey Inward Begins with Silence"

Forgive.

Truly forgive.

Not for them—but for your future.

Because you can't walk into your purpose while dragging pain behind you.

Sit With This Thought

• Are your emotions guiding your decisions—or clouding your clarity?

• Have you mistaken resentment for personality?

• What would your life look like if you truly released what happened?

Try This Within

"The Journey Inward Begins with Silence"

Blind Spot Check:

Write down three things about your past that still affect how you treat people today.

Then ask: Have I truly seen this for what it was—or only through how it felt?

Emotional Detour:

Next time you feel yourself acting out of emotion, pause.

Say aloud: "This is not who I am. This is something I'm feeling."

Then choose your response from a higher place.

CHAPTER TWENTY

"The Journey Inward Begins with Silence"

The Last Argument: You vs. Me

<u>The Seeking</u>

What if the battle you've been fighting all along wasn't with the world... but with yourself?

You can't become higher until you've outgrown the version of you that settled for lower.

There's a moment when ego must die—for truth to rise.

<u>The Mirror</u>

You vs. Me

"The Journey Inward Begins with Silence"

The war doesn't start outside—it starts in thought.

The moment you accept a lie as true, a feeling forms.

And when that feeling becomes your identity, ego is born.

Ego protects the lie.

Defends the emotion.

And fights anything that tries to correct it—even you.

But when you challenge that emotion, you challenge ego.

And when ego dies, truth lives.

I've started asking why—over and over again.

Why do I feel this?

Why do I think that?

"The Journey Inward Begins with Silence"

But the truth is… there's never a clear answer.

Because thoughts are layered.

They don't come from a single place.

They come from stories, triggers, traumas.

And once you realize there's no root,

the weeds begin to die.

Last night during prayer, something happened.

I felt a current run through my mind.

Like a wire being pulled from one side of my brain to the other.

It pulsed—like something was reprogramming me.

"The Journey Inward Begins with Silence"

It was as if my mind was transferring information from pain to peace.

I was being rewired in real time.

But the moment that scared me most?

I heard a voice…

Not mine.

It cursed me.

It took me over.

I felt possessed.

"The Journey Inward Begins with Silence"

My voice, my thoughts, my actions—none of them were mine.

It was like something used me to act out everything I never wanted to be.

And afterward, I knew:

That wasn't some random breakdown.

That was spiritual warfare.

It wasn't me vs. the world.

It was me vs. me.

Me vs. ego.

Me vs. darkness.

Me vs. fear.

"The Journey Inward Begins with Silence"

But I'm still here.

And that means I won.

<u>The Guide</u>

Secret Truths

I dream about land.

A home.

Fruit trees.

A place for family.

But sometimes I wonder—

Is it just wishful thinking?

"The Journey Inward Begins with Silence"

Is that vision what I really want?

Or is it just what I tell myself I'm supposed to want?

Because real peace doesn't come from land.

It comes from within.

I know this much:

I don't want negativity in my life anymore.

I don't want to be around it.

And I don't want to be the one creating it.

Because negativity spreads—quietly, like smoke.

And before you know it, your whole life is cloudy.

"The Journey Inward Begins with Silence"

It's scary how easy it is to change your entire mind off one moment.

One statement.

One emotion.

One lie you believe long enough to start living as truth.

But change doesn't happen from what you see—

It happens from what you face.

You can't find something you keep looking over.

And you'll never correct what you refuse to call a mistake.

Some thoughts aren't meant to be pushed down.

"The Journey Inward Begins with Silence"

They're meant to be written.

Because once it's on paper, it's real.

It can't hide anymore.

And when truth is revealed—it can finally be healed.

Sit With This Thought

• What thought are you still protecting with emotion?

• Who would you be without the version of you that's built on fear?

• Are your dreams truly yours—or borrowed from someone else's expectation?

Try This Within

"The Journey Inward Begins with Silence"

Ego Exposure:

Pick one strong emotion from this week.

Ask yourself:

• What thought created this?

• What would happen if I challenged it?

• Is this truly mine—or is this the ego defending pain?

Truth Activation:

Write a letter from your higher self to your current self.

No lies. No fear.

Just truth.

Let it speak. Then read it back—and listen.

CHAPTER TWENTY-ONE

The Way You Move Tells the Truth

<u>The Seeking</u>

If your words disappeared, would your actions still testify to your healing?

You don't have to preach peace—if you live it.

Real growth is silent. But undeniable.

<u>The Mirror</u>

Actions Speak Louder Than Words

"The Journey Inward Begins with Silence"

I'm watching my life shift right in front of me.

Not in big dramatic scenes.

But in subtle rewrites—

How I speak.

How I respond.

What I no longer chase.

As I move toward light, I notice something:

Others start shifting too.

Not because I said anything.

Not because I tried to convince them.

"The Journey Inward Begins with Silence"

But because truth, when lived fully, becomes contagious.

Still—I don't take credit for that.

I can't.

Everything good in my life?

That's God.

And everything I've stumbled through?

That's the other one.

But even in the struggle, I trust Him.

There are moments I think:

"The Journey Inward Begins with Silence"

"Once I forgive my father, I should feel peace."

But life doesn't work like that.

Peace isn't a guarantee.

It's a reward of surrender.

So instead of waiting for the feeling,

I walk in faith.

I live in prayer—not performance.

Because peace isn't proven through behavior.

It flows naturally when your heart is aligned.

People love to say:

"The Journey Inward Begins with Silence"

"Practice what you preach."

But truth is, if you're practicing it—

You don't have to preach it.

Real belief shows up in behavior.

Not in words.

Not in posts.

Not in sermons.

Who you are shows when the performance ends.

That's when the true self steps forward—

Not the version you rehearsed,

"The Journey Inward Begins with Silence"

But the one you've been healing.

Even the Bible itself tells you:

God wrote His word on your heart.

Not on pages.

Not in ink.

So why do we still treat the book like it's the only access point?

The acronym hits different now:

B.I.B.L.E. — Basic Instructions Before Leaving Earth.

But the most important instructions?

"The Journey Inward Begins with Silence"

They're already inside you.

They always were.

The Guide

Aftermath (Forgiveness Pt. 1)

You think.

You feel.

You react.

Then you suffer.

And once you suffer, you either overcome—

Or you die.

"The Journey Inward Begins with Silence"

Today, I overcame.

For the first time… I lived.

I forgave my mother.

I'd rehearsed it a hundred times in my head—

Imagined her yelling, denying, blaming me.

But when it actually happened?

She cried.

And I almost couldn't speak.

It was like something tried to choke my truth.

"The Journey Inward Begins with Silence"

Hold back my release.

But I said it anyway.

And when I did—my body emptied.

My mind cleared.

I didn't feel judgment.

I didn't feel anger.

Just peace.

True peace.

The kind that makes you forget what pain felt like.

And with that forgiveness…

"The Journey Inward Begins with Silence"

I became someone new.

It's like old desires started falling off me.

I didn't want to run anymore.

Didn't want to numb.

Didn't want to chase validation.

I just wanted to be.

Because love—real love—has no performance to it.

It doesn't scream.

It doesn't keep receipts.

It doesn't buy or prove or post.

"The Journey Inward Begins with Silence"

It just is.

And once you forgive, you see that.

You see how every conflict in life was just a misunderstanding—

Rooted in two people defending what they didn't fully understand.

Once you let go of defense,

You realize you were protecting nothing.

And that's what love really is:

Acceptance of what is.

"The Journey Inward Begins with Silence"

No emotion.

No condition.

Just truth.

Sit With This Thought

• Are your actions preaching a message your words can't explain?

• Have you forgiven with your mouth—or with your body, your behavior, your silence?

• Is your peace still conditional—or has it become who you are?

Try This Within

Silent Sermon:

"The Journey Inward Begins with Silence"

For one full day—no explaining, no defending.

Let every move you make be an act of alignment.

Let the way you walk be your proof.

Forgiveness Audit:

Pick one person you've said you forgave.

Ask yourself:

• Do my actions match that?

• Have I truly released them—or am I still reacting to them?

Write what you find. Adjust if needed.

CHAPTER TWENTY-TWO

"The Journey Inward Begins with Silence"

The Language of Awareness

The Seeking

Are you truly confused—or just unaware of how God speaks?

Sometimes clarity isn't given—it's revealed.

And you only hear what's divine when you silence what's not.

The Mirror

Simply Complexity

I think a lot.

Not out loud—but in depth.

"The Journey Inward Begins with Silence"

My mind is complex.

So is everyone else's, I imagine.

But I can't deny... sometimes I feel like I see things clearer than most.

Not better.

Just differently.

Inside, I feel like I know more than I can say.

Like my understanding of the world runs deeper than what words allow.

It's not arrogance.

It's presence.

"The Journey Inward Begins with Silence"

I pay attention.

I observe.

And because of that, I discern from a place others often overlook.

Still, I ask myself:

Who am I, really?

If I judged myself by others' opinions, I'd be a mixture of contradictions.

Some call me insightful.

Others call me difficult.

But none of those names define me.

"The Journey Inward Begins with Silence"

They're just reflections—fragments—based on what someone saw in a moment.

And if people only see me through their lens…

Then who sees me for me?

The truth is…

Most people never meet the real you.

They meet their perception of you.

Based on how they feel.

What they've experienced.

What they fear.

And I've realized I don't take offense anymore—because I don't take ownership of their lens.

"The Journey Inward Begins with Silence"

By the world's standards, I'm just another name.

Another paycheck.

Another tenant in a system I didn't create.

But through God's eyes?

I'm something else entirely.

Every month I somehow survive bills that outweigh my income.

Not because I planned well—

But because grace covered me.

That's not random.

"The Journey Inward Begins with Silence"

That's divine design.

And if you really pay attention, you'll see it too.

The world calls me average.

But God?

He's calling me something else.

The Guide

The Voice of God

People say "God spoke to me" like it's a sentence.

But how do you know?

"The Journey Inward Begins with Silence"

What does His voice even sound like?

Is it audible?

Is it a whisper in your spirit?

Is it a van driving by with a sign in the window that says, "Keep doing prayers, it works"?

Because that happened to me.

I was in the car with my girl.

Hadn't prayed in days.

I was drifting again.

Mentally checked out.

Then she pulled into the left lane and I looked to the right—

"The Journey Inward Begins with Silence"

There it was.

A message in the window of a van: Keep doing prayers, it works.

That wasn't coincidence.

That was correction.

I pointed it out.

She said, "You do that already though, so you good."

But I hadn't been.

That moment pulled me back.

That's how God talks.

"The Journey Inward Begins with Silence"

Not with thunder.

But with timing.

You can't go to Him unless you're called.

And the call doesn't always sound like church.

Sometimes it sounds like quiet.

Like something nudging your spirit when you're too tired to care.

Like a coincidence that happens too often to ignore.

Like seeing both God and the enemy in the same breath—then choosing who to follow.

It's subtle.

But it's real.

"The Journey Inward Begins with Silence"

The world teaches a set of truths based on repetition.

But God teaches through revelation.

And once you've been called,

you stop asking for signs—

because you become the sign.

Sit With This Thought

• Have you been missing divine signs because they didn't come how you expected?

• Are you listening for a loud voice, when God is whispering through your life?

• If your mind is too busy to hear, how will your spirit ever respond?

"The Journey Inward Begins with Silence"

<u>Try This Within</u>

Awareness Training:

For one day, treat everything like a sign.

That song. That license plate. That stranger's words.

Ask: What could this be pointing me to?

Write down what stands out.

Name Audit:

Write down every label you've accepted about yourself from others.

Then ask: Does this reflect who I am—or how they felt?

Keep only the truths. Release the rest.

"The Journey Inward Begins with Silence"

CHAPTER TWENTY-THREE

The Illusion of Control

<u>The Seeking</u>

If you're not in control of your thoughts, your reactions, or
your next breath—then who is?

There's wisdom in surrender.

Not because you're weak—

But because you finally realized you were never meant to do
it alone.

"The Journey Inward Begins with Silence"

<u>The Mirror</u>

Willful Control

There's good in everything.

But the bad usually overshadows it.

Good cops. Bad cops.

But somehow, the bad defines the whole.

Same with government.

Same with religion.

Same with us—human beings.

The Lord doesn't see us as we pretend to be.

"The Journey Inward Begins with Silence"

He sees us as we are:

Broken. Flawed. Capable of both light and darkness.

I sat and prayed.

Nothing deep—just a moment.

I asked the Lord to move something.

Anything.

Five minutes later, I stood up and turned on a fan.

That may sound small.

Insignificant.

But when you're sick, when you're cold, when you don't have the energy to even move—

"The Journey Inward Begins with Silence"

That's not just motion.

That's divine will being activated.

In that moment, I thanked Him.

Because I knew… it wasn't just me.

Life is strange.

But the mind? Even stranger.

When I prayed, I could see clearer.

Not with my eyes—but with something deeper.

My spirit moved my body before my sight could catch up.

I couldn't feel my hands or feet.

"The Journey Inward Begins with Silence"

It was light—like truth wrapped around me.

Like presence itself had taken form inside me.

And it hit me:

If He's in me,

Then anything I want or need…

I can ask for.

The desire to move doesn't even come from me.

It's given.

It's planted.

And when I align with Him,

even small movements—like turning on a fan—become sacred.

"The Journey Inward Begins with Silence"

That's not superstition.

That's awareness.

So I asked God:

"Help me pray to You at least twice a day.

Once when I rise.

Once before I rest."

Because prayer isn't just words.

It's access.

It's calibration.

It's movement that starts where eyes can't see.

"The Journey Inward Begins with Silence"

<u>The Guide</u>

Works of Wisdom

I'm chasing something quieter these days.

Not success.

Not recognition.

Just a sound mind.

A place where no thoughts hijack my peace.

Where I don't wrestle with distractions.

Where silence becomes sacred again.

If evil is real—and I've seen it—

"The Journey Inward Begins with Silence"

Then good must be real too.

That's logic.

But deeper than logic, I feel it.

I want to be one of the good ones.

Not performatively.

But genuinely.

Inside and out.

So I rejoice.

Even when I don't understand.

Because I've learned—

You don't worry your way into blessings.

You pray your way into them.

"The Journey Inward Begins with Silence"

I got a $300 check out of nowhere.

Some might say luck.

But I know better.

There's no such thing as coincidence.

Only divine math.

Everything is action and reaction.

Calculated.

Precise.

Purposeful.

I had a daydream once—

Men lining up at heaven's gates, holding their wife's hand.

"The Journey Inward Begins with Silence"

One by one, they stepped forward.

If God approved the marriage, they walked through the gate.

Their rug continued into paradise.

But if He denied it?

The gates slammed shut.

The rug pulled from beneath them.

Their wife handcuffed herself to them, and they were dragged straight into hell.

That's what it feels like when we build things without God's blessing.

We call it love.

We call it fate.

"The Journey Inward Begins with Silence"

But we never asked the One who created both.

I've come to realize…

Most people are the walking dead.

Not because they're evil.

But because they think they're in control.

They're being tricked.

Same way I was.

Same way you might be.

So I say this:

Look at yourself.

Overcome yourself.

"The Journey Inward Begins with Silence"

Forgive yourself.

Forget yourself.

Because in truth—

You never made yourself to begin with.

Sit With This Thought

• Have you confused free will with control?

• What in your life are you trying to manage that's not yours
to carry?

• What's one moment in your life that proves divine
intervention is real?

Try This Within

"The Journey Inward Begins with Silence"

Power Audit:

Write down 3 things you're trying to control right now.

Then ask:

• Have I invited God into this?

• What would surrender look like here?

Prayer Rewire:

Start and end your next 3 days with one sentence of honest prayer.

Not performance.

Just honesty.

See what shifts—not in the world, but in you.

CHAPTER TWENTY-FOUR

Letting Go of the Want

<u>The Seeking</u>

Are you seeking purpose—or trying to earn something you were already born with?

True freedom doesn't come from finding meaning.

It comes from no longer needing meaning to be whole.

<u>The Mirror</u>

New Understandings

"The Journey Inward Begins with Silence"

When you start walking differently—

People start falling away.

Not everyone can go with you.

Not because you don't love them—

But because they were only meant to understand who you were.

Not who you're becoming.

And I had to ask myself:

Were they ever really with me?

Or were they just present while I stayed silent?

Truth is…

"The Journey Inward Begins with Silence"

Before any of this—before the trauma, the confusion, the inner war—

I was already known.

Already guided.

In my mother's womb, before I had words,

I was protected.

I didn't think.

I didn't perform.

I just was.

And somehow, I never drowned.

Somehow, I lived.

That's not luck.

"The Journey Inward Begins with Silence"

That's divine.

Nowadays, people approach me with their own expectations.

They see something in me and want it for themselves.

But after a conversation, they leave different.

Maybe they don't speak to me again—

But I know the seed was planted.

And I don't speak from theory.

I speak from life.

Because I'm guided.

Not by fear.

"The Journey Inward Begins with Silence"

Not by ego.

But by God.

And because I've stopped judging,

I've learned how to love everybody.

When you walk in light,

you see darkness.

And once you see it,

God starts removing it from around you.

Not because you're perfect.

But because you're ready to stop pretending to be broken.

"The Journey Inward Begins with Silence"

The battle isn't physical.

It's spiritual.

And now that I know that—

I don't fight it anymore.

I flow through it.

The Guide

No Need to Want Purpose

Sometimes when I pray, I feel like I'm on the outside looking in—

like my spirit is watching my body go through the motions of a life I'm still trying to understand.

"The Journey Inward Begins with Silence"

Other times, my mind plays tricks.

I start praying, and suddenly I'm falling asleep.

My thoughts wander—

Not to revelations, but to nonsense.

Dreams that hold no weight.

Thoughts that lead nowhere.

It's like something is trying to keep me from the one thing that feeds my soul.

And I realize… most people don't really know what they want or need.

That's why, when they finally get it, they keep reaching for more.

The want never ends.

"The Journey Inward Begins with Silence"

The need never sleeps.

Because they're not chasing the thing—

They're chasing the feeling.

But feelings lie.

They move.

They fade.

They betray.

Today, I thought about how we treat our kids when trying to teach them something.

How patient are we when they're frustrated?

When they're tired?

"The Journey Inward Begins with Silence"

When they say, "I can't"?

I was teaching my son to count.

To him, it felt like I was keeping him from candy.

To me, I was teaching him discipline.

Delayed gratification.

Self-mastery.

He saw it as punishment.

But I saw it as purpose.

He thought I was being mean.

But I was really being loving.

"The Journey Inward Begins with Silence"

And that's how God moves.

He's not withholding blessings.

He's shaping us to carry them.

My son will learn—just like I am:

When you master yourself,

you get what you want.

Not because you beg for it,

but because you're ready to receive it.

<u>Sit With This Thought</u>

• Are you working for purpose—or awakening to it?

"The Journey Inward Begins with Silence"

• What's one thing you keep reaching for that's already been placed inside you?

• Can you be at peace without needing more?

Try This Within

Desire Detox:

List 5 things you "want."

Now ask yourself for each:

• Is this something I truly need?

• Is it already mine in another form?

• What would change if I stopped chasing it?

Silent Teaching:

"The Journey Inward Begins with Silence"

Spend 10 minutes today teaching someone something without using your voice.

Whether it's a child, partner, or stranger—lead by presence.

Let your patience speak louder than your words.

CHAPTER TWENTY-FIVE

God Between Thoughts

<u>The Seeking</u>

Are your thoughts guiding you—or gaslighting you?

There's a quiet voice between all the noise.

It doesn't argue.

"The Journey Inward Begins with Silence"

It doesn't beg.

It simply waits for you to stop reacting... so you can finally hear it.

The Mirror

Metatron

I was sitting in prayer when the visions came.

Not peaceful ones.

Not comforting ones.

"The Journey Inward Begins with Silence"

They were layered, chaotic—like emotional puzzles flying around me, each piece demanding attention.

Images of my mother.

Memories we hadn't even lived yet.

Scenarios I feared might happen.

And all of it came wrapped in guilt and anxiety, like they were trying to pull me out of the moment.

But I didn't flinch.

I stayed still.

I let God shield me.

Because when you don't react to your thoughts—

You finally realize they never had control.

"The Journey Inward Begins with Silence"

They're not you.

They're just echoes of everything you've feared, felt, or suppressed.

Even the good ones are tricky.

They give you highs just to crash you later.

They make you feel invincible today so they can shame you tomorrow.

That's why I've learned to relax in all thoughts.

The exciting ones.

The terrifying ones.

The shameful ones.

"The Journey Inward Begins with Silence"

Because the moment I react—I lose.

And that's the true spiritual war.

Not between heaven and hell.

But between you… and your own response to thought.

There was a moment in prayer when I saw it clearly—

A cube. Transparent, purplish, hovering above my head.

Inside it were the fragments of me and my mother—floating, looping, replaying.

Demonic figures stood around us. Watching.

But they couldn't touch me.

"The Journey Inward Begins with Silence"

Because God was in the stillness.

That's when I knew:

Even when the devil is loud,

God is still present.

He just doesn't shout.

The Guide

Mind to Mind

One decision affects everything that follows.

That's how real free will is.

"The Journey Inward Begins with Silence"

Every path leads somewhere.

And sometimes the wrong road is disguised as righteousness—because it fits your feelings.

I used to gamble with my choices.

Not just big ones like crime or violence.

But small ones—like being late on rent, ignoring responsibility, choosing silence over communication.

They seemed harmless at first.

But consequences came.

Always.

That's when I started asking:

Is this really right... or just familiar?

"The Journey Inward Begins with Silence"

Because some things we call "evil" might actually be the righteousness we've been avoiding—

Not because it's wrong,

but because it requires us to surrender our comfort.

When I feel someone's vibe, it hits me strong.

It shifts my energy.

Sometimes it makes me uneasy.

Other times, peaceful.

And I wonder—

Is this just emotional projection?

"The Journey Inward Begins with Silence"

Or are we really feeling each other, mind to mind?

I think we are.

Some people speak without words.

They send signals.

Their pain speaks louder than their voice.

I feel that with my son.

There's a spiritual connection between us I can't explain.

It's not just love.

It's a frequency.

"The Journey Inward Begins with Silence"

He doesn't have to say it—

I know when he's hurting.

I feel it like my own.

That's when I realized…

Our souls are connected beyond explanation.

The worry I feel about him isn't mine alone.

It's shared.

And that means…

The healing can be shared too.

When I lift myself, I lift him.

"The Journey Inward Begins with Silence"

When I calm my mind, I calm his future.

It's not just about me anymore.

Sit With This Thought

• What thoughts keep trying to pull you out of peace?

• What if the confusion you feel isn't yours—but something passed down to you?

• Can you hold still long enough to hear the real voice of God—beneath the noise?

Try This Within

Reaction Fast:

For one day, don't react to your thoughts.

"The Journey Inward Begins with Silence"

Whatever comes—observe it. Don't fight it. Don't follow it. Just witness.

At the end of the day, ask yourself: What stayed with me? What faded?

Mind-to-Mind Prayer:

Think of someone you love deeply—your child, your partner, your parent.

Sit still. No words. Just breathe.

Imagine peace flowing from your chest into theirs.

Visualize them receiving it.

That's prayer beyond language.

CHAPTER TWENTY-SIX

"The Journey Inward Begins with Silence"

The Final Voice Before Silence

The Seeking

What if every voice in your head isn't yours?

Thoughts don't ask for permission.

Some come to free you.

Some come to kill you.

The only question is—can you tell the difference?

The Mirror

When He Comes

"The Journey Inward Begins with Silence"

When he comes, he doesn't knock.

He enters through thought.

Through feeling.

Through a moment you didn't even know you left the door open.

I was sitting in silence one day.

I had a thought:

"I need to go see my dad."

But that thought didn't sit still.

It moved.

It twisted.

"The Journey Inward Begins with Silence"

It started shaping a scene in my head—one that ended in violence.

In that daydream, we fought.

I had him in an armbar.

He screamed for me to let go.

And I responded with a voice I didn't even recognize.

It wasn't mine.

It came from deep inside… or maybe far below:

"FUCK YOU, NIGGA."

I felt the break in his arm.

Then snapped back into reality.

Room was quiet.

"The Journey Inward Begins with Silence"

Nobody was around.

Just me—and what had used me.

That's the terrifying part.

I wasn't angry.

I wasn't depressed.

But those thoughts—

homicidal, suicidal, perverted—

they came anyway.

Not from pain.

But from somewhere else.

Somewhere that doesn't need a reason to invade.

"The Journey Inward Begins with Silence"

That's when I realized:

I don't have control.

At least, not in the way I thought.

The voice that whispers now isn't mine.

It mocks me.

It tries to convince me to do things I know are wrong.

And sometimes…

It laughs through me.

There are moments I feel myself smiling or laughing—

and I don't even know why.

That's not mental illness.

"The Journey Inward Begins with Silence"

That's spiritual invasion.

Possession isn't always Hollywood.

Sometimes, it's daydreaming.

Sometimes, it's being talked into hating someone for no reason.

Sometimes, it's hearing a voice that sounds like yours…

but it only ever brings chaos.

That's how he comes.

Subtle.

Internal.

Uninvited.

"The Journey Inward Begins with Silence"

But once you know he's there—

You've already started winning.

The Guide

When You Know

I started asking myself questions that most people avoid.

Like—can he use the information I learn against me?

And if so, is that how the devil keeps people stuck?

By tricking them into overthinking truth?

"The Journey Inward Begins with Silence"

I wondered if I was being manipulated through the very things that once freed me.

What if the voice that sounds like growth… is still him?

Or maybe…

just maybe…

there's a real voice of me buried beneath all the others.

The true self.

The higher self.

The one that was mine before trauma, before possession, before confusion.

I write to find that voice.

To strip away what isn't mine.

"The Journey Inward Begins with Silence"

To document the difference between what I feel… and what I know.

Because I'm learning now:

Just because I feel something—

doesn't mean it's truth.

Emotion is not fact.

And thoughts are not instructions.

Every feeling isn't real.

Some are rehearsed.

Some are borrowed.

Some are straight-up lies planted in the soil of our minds.

"The Journey Inward Begins with Silence"

So now I watch them.

I study my thoughts like parables.

Decode them instead of following them.

That's how I build faith.

Not by shouting.

Not by begging.

But by watching quietly until I can tell who's talking.

Because once you know...

You never unknow.

"The Journey Inward Begins with Silence"

And once you stop reacting—

You start becoming.

Sit With This Thought

• Have you ever mistaken a voice in your head as your own, when it wasn't?

• If peace has a sound, do you recognize it?

• Could your "normal" thoughts actually be your deepest form of spiritual warfare?

Try This Within

Possession Check:

Sit in silence for 10 minutes.

"The Journey Inward Begins with Silence"

Let all thoughts come and go—but do not respond.

Write down the first thought that demanded your reaction.

Ask: Was this me? Or something using me?

Voice Fast:

For one day, every time you hear your inner voice say "I," replace it with "the voice said…"

Observe how that shift changes your relationship with thought.

Do it for a full day. Journal what you notice.

CHAPTER TWENTY-SEVEN

Sitting With Your Thoughts

"The Journey Inward Begins with Silence"

<u>The Final Journal Entry</u>: (Complete Integration of All 52 Journal Entries)

I sat… and I thought.

I asked questions to it—

not knowing what "it" was at first,

just that I had to ask.

So I put my Cards on the Table, and what came next…

wasn't silence.

It was a Voice from Above.

"The Journey Inward Begins with Silence"

But it wasn't just above.

It was inside me, speaking Mind to Mind.

It made me Face Reality,

and I realized—

this entire time, I'd been fighting a War on Thoughts.

Because When You Know, you can't pretend you don't.

You can't unsee it.

You can't lie to yourself anymore.

So I wrote my Message to God,

asking for clarity.

Asking for purpose.

Asking for peace.

"The Journey Inward Begins with Silence"

And the reply?

It wasn't what I expected.

It was a story,

a parable wrapped in Secret Truths.

It said:

Your Brain Works,

but only when you stop trying to think.

Your thoughts don't create your soul.

The Birth of the Spirit starts in surrender.

And When He Comes,

he doesn't knock.

"The Journey Inward Begins with Silence"

He slips in.

Subtle.

Quiet.

Until one day he's Knockin on Your Front Door,

wearing faces you once trusted.

But even then,

you're still the Dreamer.

He Planted Seeds,

filled with Emotional Temptation.

That's how he keeps you Casually Normal.

"The Journey Inward Begins with Silence"

He'll dim your Light in View

until you forget it was ever there.

Because when the Devil Presents,

it don't always come with horns—

sometimes it comes with charm.

And when it does…

your sight becomes Twenty Twenty,

but backwards.

Still, in my Forgiveness Pt. 1,

I found the first key.

I started learning the Learning Ways,

walked Clear Pathways,

"The Journey Inward Begins with Silence"

and followed the steps toward the Fate of Faith.

Through every mistake,

I gained New Understandings.

I stopped fearing the Internal Darkness,

and faced the truth:

the war was always Good vs Evil,

but the battlefield was me.

The signs were everywhere.

Mental Bruising Physical,

smiles hiding scars,

confidence masking shame.

"The Journey Inward Begins with Silence"

The world tried to Judge or Discern me,

but only God knew what peace looked like on the inside.

Even Drugged Moments became sacred,

because they made me write.

And I realized…

my Actions Speak Louder Than Words.

So when I walked through those Dark Hallways,

I walked quiet.

I faced every Thought of Doubting Thoughts,

found Deep Truths in my own contradictions,

"The Journey Inward Begins with Silence"

and listened for Mental Guidance

in the quiet.

Because even in Simply Complexity,

the voice of truth is never complicated.

It's buried in History Memories,

hidden beneath trauma,

wrapped in Issues of Trust.

But healing ain't linear.

Forgiveness Pt. 2 taught me that.

Sometimes Relationship Tricks

"The Journey Inward Begins with Silence"

will break you open.

Sometimes you'll start Living Inside Out,

grabbing hold of Willful Control

just to feel stable again.

But in truth—

you have to become Oblivious to Life

to start seeing it for what it really is.

You have to be willing

to observe your Thought to See,

to feel the Thought to Feel,

and still say—

"The Journey Inward Begins with Silence"

I have No Need to Want Purpose.

Because purpose comes

when you finally stop asking for one.

Purpose is peace.

And peace…

comes when you're Sitting With Your Thoughts.

The Becoming

No more searching.

No more answers.

No more fighting your reflection in the mirror.

"The Journey Inward Begins with Silence"

You've come home.

Everything you were looking for was already within.

Every voice. Every test. Every twist.

All of it brought you here—

to the stillness.

To the silence.

To yourself.

Welcome back.

REVIEW

"The Journey Inward Begins with Silence"

Sitting With Your Thoughts is a literary and spiritual triumph. Malik's raw, poetic voice transforms trauma into testimony, inner dialogue into divine reflection. Across 27 immersive chapters, the reader walks through chaos, silence, spiritual confrontation, and eventual peace. The structure, deeply introspective and grounded in real experience, feels like scripture for the soul-accessible, unforgettable, and necessary. Malik doesn't preach-he awakens. This is more than a memoir—it's a guidebook for the spiritually restless. A rare, honest, and masterful work destined to be remembered.